FLICKER BIBLE STUDY

DESIRE-POWERED INDUCTIVE BIBLE STUDY

Noel and Denise Enete

WAVE
Study
Bible

Published by WAVE Study Bible, Inc.
WaveStudyBible.com
Edition 3.5.1

Scripture quotations noted **NIV** are taken from the *HOLY BIBLE, NEW INTERNATIONAL VERSION*.
Copyright 1973, 1978, and 1984 by International Bible Society. Used by permission of Zondervan Publishing
House. All rights reserved.

Scripture quotations noted **NASB** are taken from the *NEW AMERICAN STANDARD BIBLE*, Copyright 1960,
1962, 1963, 1968, 1971, 1972, 1973, 1975, 1977, by The Lockman Foundation. Used by permission.

The FLCR study strategy was adapted from Anne Graham Lotz's *Living a Life that is Blessed*, Copyright 1995
by AnGel Ministries.

Cover by graphic artist and jazz musician Dorothy Collins Wineman

ISBN 978-0-9791595-5-8

Printed and bound in the United States of America

Table of Contents

Chapters

Desire and Discipline   13

Motivation for Reading 13

Learning to See 21

Assignment 1 27

Uncovering Your Desire   31

Review Motivation Assignment 1 34

Desire Squasher: Deceitful Desires 34

What Do You Want? 39

Review Skill Assignment 1 41

Flicker Bible Study 41

Flicker Practice 49

Assignment 2 57

Renewing Your Mind   61

Review Motivation Assignment 2 62

How We Think Effects How We feel 63

How We Think Effects How We Grow 67

What Do You Want? 70

Desire Squasher: Futile Thinking 73

Review Skill Assignment 2 75

Help with Finding the Lessons 76

Assignment 3 83

Independence or Walking Toward God?   87

Review Motivation Assignment 3 87

Independence from God 89

God's Help 90

Desire Squasher: Taking Offense 95

Review Skill Assignment 3 98

Flicker Practice 99

About Flicker Practice 104

Assignment 4 105

Removing Thorns   109

Review Motivation Assignment 4 110
Family of Origin Issues 111
Family Of Origin Issues can Distort Bible Study 113
Get to Know God 115
Identify How God Differs From Your Parents. 116
Review Skill Assignment 4 119
Flicker Practice 119
About Flicker Practice 124
Assignment 5. 125

Stretching Your Comfort Zone   129

Review Motivation Assignment 5 130
Biblical Comfort Zone Examples 131
Introverts and Extroverts. 133
Get to Know God 137
Review Skill Assignment 5 140
Flicker Practice 141
About Flicker Practice 146
Assignment 6. 147

Aligning Your Prayers   151

Review Motivation Assignment 5 152
Prayer in Three Steps. 153
Step 1: Align with God. 155
Step 2: Ask for What You Want 168
Step 3: Prepare to Receive It 178
Review Skill Assignment 6 180
Flicker Practice 181
About Flicker Practice 186
Assignment 7. 187

Pacing Your Growth   191

Review Motivation Assignment 7 192
Testimony. 193

God Loves Small Beginnings 196

Review Skill Assignment 7 198

Flicker Practice 199

About Flicker Practice 204

Conclusion 205

Appendix

Promises   209

Guidance 209

Forgiveness 209

Sickness. 210

Trouble 210

Marriage 211

Children 212

Safety. 213

Need for Success or Prosperity. 213

God Keeps His Promises. 215

Answers   217

Reminder Card   235

How Well Do You See?   239

More Help with Finding the Lessons   245

Answering Your Questions   249

Finding the Time   257

Designing a Time With God   263

More About the Authors   271

"For I am
the Lord, your God,
who takes hold
of your right hand
and says to you,
'Do not fear;
I will help you.'"

Isa 41:13 (NIV)

Preface

One misty Saturday morning several years ago I [N] was sitting on my surfboard at a local surf spot waiting for a wave with my kids. The surf was small that day and everybody in the water was waiting for the next wave in silence.

When the wave came, I noticed a very small boy, who didn't know how to surf, attempt to catch the wave. He did not know the basics of surfing and was not in the right place to catch the wave nor was he balanced on the surfboard to paddle efficiently. So he missed or got clobbered by most of the waves he tried to catch.

His father stood on the shore—fully clothed and dry. As a wave approached, his father would boom out commands to his struggling son, "Turn around. Paddle! Paddle Harder! You could have gotten that. You've got to try harder!" The father's voice echoed up and down the beach and must have embarrassed the young boy.

After a while, the surfers started exchanging knowing glances of sympathy for the boy's plight. So, I turned to my kids and asked what the father should be doing. They said the father should be in the water—next to his son—helping him succeed rather than shouting commands from a distance.

Many Quiet Time books stand on the shore and shout commands to their struggling readers from a distance. We don't do that.

Just like catching a wave depends on the proper functioning of interrelated skills, developing a successful Bible reading time depends on the balancing of several skills like the improvement of your ability to study the Bible, the negotiation with your motivation, and the management of your time.

Which of these skills to focus on and which to lead with, make all the difference between catching a wave or just getting tired and giving up.

In this journey, we get in the water with you. We help you uncover the *Desire* God has given you to be with Him. At the same time we guide you through a few simple steps that make Bible reading easier.

By carefully reinforcing your *Desire* for God, at the same time as enhancing your Bible study skill, you develop an approach to Bible reading that you look forward to and that you keep wanting to do.

If you decide to take this journey and do the assignments, rest assured your life will never be the same.

Organization of the Book

Each chapter has a section to strengthen your *Motivation* and a section to develop your Bible reading *Skill*.

The assignment at the end of each chapter has a *Motivation* section and a *Skill* section. If you get stuck, the answers for the assignments can be found in the Appendix titled *Answers*.

The eight chapters can be covered one per week when using the book as curriculum in a small group.

Feedback

If you would like to contact us, we love to hear from our readers.

noel.enete@wavestudybible.com
denise.enete@wavestudybible.com

Drs. Noel and Denise Enete
Irvine, California
October, 2019

(our last name is pronounced eee NET)

Enjoy your adventure as you explore the rich and living word of God.

Chapters

"Discipline
can smooth out
the bumps in a road,
but it can not
make the road."

The Authors

Chapter 1
Desire and Discipline

"I think I have to break the door down," Jack blustered.

"Wait! Surely there is another way," his wife countered. But Jack was determined. He had locked them out of their mobile home and was sure this was their only option.

"I'll go around and see if I can get in some other way," his wife offered. But Jack was busy preparing his assault. After a couple of moments, he decided to let it rip and exploded through the front door.

As he lay on the demolished door, his wife came walking down the hall and said dryly, "The back door was open."

I [N] had to laugh when Jack (changed name) recounted the demise of his front door to a group of us. But it is all too common for Christians to take the same approach toward their Bible reading. When their motivation for reading weakens, they think their only option is to mow down their feelings and force themselves through the activity.

If you address your Bible reading the way Jack addressed his front door, it won't be long before you are lying on a demolished Time with God. If you are already there, Denise and I are walking down the hall to tell you God provides a better way.

Motivation for Reading

It may surprise you, but the motivation that moves you to read the Bible colors what you get out of it. At the two extremes, you either sit down to read the Bible because you *want* to (*Desire-led*), or because you think you *should* (*Discipline-led*).

1. There are two approaches to having a time with God:

Desire -led

Discipline -led

Healthy Bible reading involves both *Desire* and *Discipline* but it is very important which one you lead with.

Bible reading is not the same as doing a homework assignment in school. Usually the objective in school homework is to acquire some information. But the objective in reading the Bible is to enrich your relationship with God and be transformed. *Discipline* is sufficient motivation to acquire facts, but not for changing a heart.

Effective Bible reading begins with your motivation.

Desire-led or Discipline-led?

The *Desire-led* approach says the way to read the Bible effectively is to uncover and nurture the *Desire* God has given you to be with Him, then read the Bible because you *want* to be a little closer to Him.

The *Discipline-led* approach says you can not count on feelings and that you should read your Bible at the scheduled time regardless how you feel. Don't make any adjustments to your schedule. Don't make sure the time and frequency match your current *Desire*. Just keep pushing through your Bible reading times regardless.

It is true that sometimes you will not feel like sitting down and spending Time with God at the scheduled moment. But if you uncover the *Desire* God has given you, and build your Bible reading time around that, you can get through those rough spots with much less *Discipline*.

Discipline can smooth out the bumps in a road, but it can not build the road.

Having said that, *Discipline-led* Bible reading can work. You might start out with *Discipline* then get caught up with who God is and end up wanting to spend time with Him. But there are hazards with the *Discipline-led* approach.

If you happen to be *good* at *Discipline*, it is tempting to get a bit smug about checking off Bible reading from your "to do" list regularly when others can't seem to get to theirs. The danger is operating independently of God—you don't really need Him. You are just proudly performing for Him.

On the other hand, if you happen to *not* be good at *Discipline*, you can quickly become disheartened and discouraged because you can't make yourself be consistent.

Surprisingly at that point, I [D] think the disheartened and discouraged person is closer to pleasing God than the smug one. At least the disheartened person knows they need God whereas the proud performer is content to operate independently from Him.

Balanced Bible reading includes both *Desire* and *Discipline*. But it is important that you lead with your *Desire*. That is how God equipped you and that will put you in the best place to succeed.

Example: Martha and Mary

The story of Martha and Mary in *Luke 10* contrasts the *Desire-led* and *Discipline-led* approaches to devotion.

For a long time I [D] did not like the story of Martha and Mary in the Bible. Especially around the holidays when I would spend extra time and effort baking, cooking special meals, decorating, and cleaning. I would do these things in service of the family, but it seemed like this Bible passage minimized my efforts. Then God gave me a better understanding. The story is in *Luke 10:38-42*.

> *Luke 10:38-42 As Jesus and his disciples were on their way, he came to a village where a woman named* **Martha** *opened her home to him. She had a sister called* **Mary,** *who sat at the Lord's feet listening to what he said. But Martha was distracted by all the preparations that had to be made. She came to him and asked, "Lord, don't you care that my sister has left me to do the work by myself?* **Tell her to help me!"** *"Martha, Martha," the Lord answered, "you are worried and upset about many things, but only one thing is needed.* **Mary has chosen what is better,** *and it will not be taken away from her." (NIV1984)*

You can imagine how Martha and Mary were excited! Jesus was going to be a guest in their home. Martha thought, "Jesus is coming to my home, how can I please Him? I know, I'll make Him a beautiful meal. Then He will know how much I love Him."

On the other hand Mary thought, "Jesus is going to be a guest in our home, how can I please Him? I know. I'll just be with Him. I'll sit at His feet and dote on Him. I'll hang on His every word then He will know how much I love Him."

Martha had more of a *Discipline-led* focus. She was focused on herself—how she could serve and what she could give. Mary was more *Desire-led* with her focus more on Jesus and what she could learn from Him. As we see from the story, Mary had her fingers on Jesus' pulse.

The *Discipline-led* approach to devotion is sort of like a husband who buys his wife tires for her birthday. He is being generous and it is good for him to provide for her safety. But a birthday is a special time when everyone focuses on a person to show them how special they are. New tires may not be a good way to show a wife how special she is to her husband. Instead, if he were to say, "Your birthday is coming up and I would just love to spend time with you. How about if I take you to a beautiful hotel and just treat you?" Most women would love that gift.

I think the reason the Martha and Mary story made it into the Bible, is that Jesus is a guest in our hearts. How are we going to please Him? Are we going to focus on ourselves and what we can do for Him, or are we going to focus on Him and what we can learn from Him? We will certainly *do* things for Him but where is our focus?

Don't you know that if Martha had gone to Jesus and said, "I'm not sure what to do. I want to make you a beautiful meal, but I also want to be with you. What should I do?" Something tells me that Jesus could have helped her. If He fed 5,000, don't you know He could have handled 12 or so? Martha missed the chance to be with Him.

Example: Jesus and the Father

Mary is not the only Bible character that lead with *Desire*. Jesus acts on His *Desire* to be with His Father as described in *Hebrews 1:3,13*.

There are many things that are significant about Jesus sitting at the right hand of the Father, but don't miss the significance of the fellowship they were having. Jesus is spending time just being with the Father.

Hebrews 1:3,13 The Son is the radiance of God's glory and the exact representation of his being, sustaining all things *by his powerful word. After he had provided purification for sins, he sat down **at the right hand of the Majesty in heaven** ... To which of the angels did God ever say, "**Sit at my right hand** until I make your enemies a footstool for your feet?" (NIV1984)*

God values time spent in each other's company.

Deeds and Desire

There is nothing wrong with good works. But leading with them will tend to smother your *Desire*. In *Revelation 2:2-5* God acknowledges the hard work and perseverance of the believers in the church of Ephesus, but He says they have fallen greatly from where they started.

> *Revelation 2:2-5 I know your deeds, **your hard work and your perseverance**. I know that you can not tolerate wicked men, that you have tested those who claim to be apostles but are not, and have found them false. You have persevered and endured hardships for my name, and have not grown weary. Yet I hold this against you: **You have forsaken your first love**. Remember the height from which you have fallen! **Repent and do the things you did at first**. (NIV1984)*

When they started, they were motivated by love and by *Desiring* a relationship with Him. He urges them to return to to their "first love" and be *Desire-led*.

God did not create us for cheap labor, as if He needed our labor *(Acts 17:24-25)*. We are not just worker bees. He could do our work so much faster and more efficiently Himself. But He allows us to blunder along, doing His work, because it is good for us.

> *Acts 17:24-25 "The God who made the world and everything in it is the Lord of heaven and earth and does not live in temples built by hands. **And he is not served by human hands, as if he needed anything,** because he himself gives all men life and breath and everything else." (NIV1984)*

If you are a parent, and you have a 5 year old child learning to tie his shoes, it is tempting to reach down and tie them when you are in a hurry. But most of the time you wait and let him tie them because it is better for him to practice and learn to do it himself.

God is patient with us. He lets us practice doing things for Him, but He wants us to focus on Him, not on our work for Him. In fact, *Revelation 3:16-21* points out the futility of thinking we are self-sufficient performers. It says rather, that we are blind, pitiful, and poor when we act independently.

> *Revelation 3:16-21 So, because you are lukewarm — neither hot nor cold — I am about to spit you out of my mouth. You say, "I am rich; I have acquired wealth and do not need a thing." But **you do not realize that you are wretched, pitiful, poor, blind and naked**. I counsel you to buy from me gold refined in the fire, so you can become rich; and white clothes to wear, so you can cover your shameful nakedness; and salve to put on your eyes so you can see. Those whom I love I rebuke and discipline. So be earnest, and repent. Here I am! I stand at the door and knock. **If anyone hears my voice and opens the door, I will come in and eat with him, and he with me.** To him who overcomes, I will give the right **to sit with me** on my throne, just as I overcame and **sat down with my Father on his throne**. (NIV1984)*

We don't need to act independently from God. He offers the fellowship we need. He is willing to let us sit down with Him on His throne.

He has given us a supernatural *Desire* for Him—the Ferrari within. But some of us settle for the tricycle of *Discipline*. We are peddling around as fast as we can, working hard with all the *Discipline* we can muster. But God values fellowship.

In our culture we *are* what we *do*. Our value is in our work. But to God, a quadriplegic is just as valuable as an able-bodied person because fellowship with God is Spirit to spirit not Spirit to resume.

It is all about following your *Desire* to have fellowship with Him.

Your God-given Desire

God equips us with the *Desires* we need. God equips an infant with a *Desire* for milk. In *1 Peter 2:2* the Bible says our *Desire* for God is like a baby's *Desire* for milk.

> *1 Peter 2:2* **Like** *newborn babies,* **crave** *pure spiritual milk, so that by it you may grow up in your salvation (NIV1984)*

If a newborn baby is healthy, he or she *Desires* milk. The baby does not need to use *Discipline* to drink the milk. So think back to when you first accepted God's gift and remember the *Desire* you felt for Him.

Consider the deer in *Psalm 42:1-2* who has a deep, natural, God-given thirst for water. God has placed the same thirst within you.

> *Psalm 42:1-2* *As the* **deer pants** *for streams of water, so* **my soul pants for you***, O God. My soul thirsts for God, for the living God. When can I go and meet with God? (NIV1984)*

These are God-given *Desires* that keep us on track. Consider the *Desire* God has placed within you. We will help you find that *Desire*, strengthen it, and guard it.

> *Matthew 5:6* *Blessed are those who hunger and thirst for righteousness,* **for they will be filled.** *(NIV1984)*

Learning to See

Each chapter in this book includes a section to help you with Bible study *Skill*. This enables you to grow your Bible *Skill* at the same time you are uncovering your God-given *Desire*.

Out of the four steps in *Flicker Bible study,* the first step is the most important—Learning to See.

This single step will do more for your ability to understand the Bible than any other single thing. Bible study is all about what you see. And fortunately, you already know how to do it.

2. Bible study is all about what you

See
_____

We see things all day long. If we see someone frowning and mumbling, we generally conclude they are upset about something. If we see someone smiling and talking quickly with animated gestures, we conclude they are excited. We regularly hone our ability to observe and learn from what we see. This same skill is the foundation of all Bible study.

Video Clip

To help you with the *Skill* of learning to *See,* take a moment to watch the *Dancer Texas* video clip. Then simply write down what you *See* (in the space provided). The video can be found on the Internet at this location:

https://youtu.be/HMJLXCZfEEU

3. What do you See in the Video Clip?

Country road
4 guys in lawn chairs
talking, one guy reading
something
slow area, no cars
coming, scattered clouds
one road sign
fencing. no animals
warm day
near an old gas station
breezy
one car drives down
the highway
old blue converible car

About the Video Clip

What did you see?

You probably noticed that there were four boys talking with each other. Could you tell anything about them by the way they were dressed? Could you tell who the leader(s) of the group were by their interaction. Who do you figure was low-man on the totem pole socially?

What kind of a town was *Dancer Texas?* Was there a lot to do or not? What do you make out of the condition of the gas station in the background? What do you make out of them sitting across the highway as they talked? What did you make out of them not being worried about the car that was coming?

About what age were these kids? How do you know? Did they attend a large school? Who was graduating today? What were their plans after graduation? Were they all equally determined to leave the town?

Look how much you learned about the video after only a few minutes. You practice this *Skill* every day. You are constantly looking at things and sizing them up… and you are good at it!

Bible Passage

That *Skill* is the core of Bible study and you already know how to do it.

On the next page you will find a few sentences from the Bible. Read the sentences and write out what you see (in the space provided).

As you read, it may help you to construct a mental picture of the scene and what is happening. Then just write down what you see in your picture.

Mark 12:41-44

Mark 12:41 And He sat down opposite the treasury, and [began] observing how the people were putting money into the treasury; and many rich people were putting in large sums.

Mark 12:42 A poor widow came and put in two small copper coins, which amount to a cent.

Mark 12:43 Calling His disciples to Him, He said to them, "Truly I say to you, this poor widow put in more than all the contributors to the treasury;

Mark 12:44 for they all put in out of their surplus, but she, out of her poverty, put in all she owned, all she had to live on." (NASB)

- Jesus sat near where the church money was
- He's watching people put money in
- Rich people put in a lot of money
- poor widow put in paltry amt
- He called his disciples over
- He says "Truly" for seriousness
- the poor put in more than the rich
- The rich put in their extra
- the poor put in everything she had

What do you See in Mark 12:41-44?

About the Bible Passage

What did you see?

Did you happen to notice that Jesus was interested in how people gave money to the treasury? Jesus mentions that rich people were giving large sums to the treasury. What do you suppose that looked like? What do you suppose they were wearing? Do you think they were meek and mild and clothed humbly or more outward and flamboyant?

When the poor widow came up to give her small amount of money, what do you suppose she looked like?—flamboyant or contrite? How do you suppose she felt as she followed the extravagant givers? Do you think she was tempted to feel embarrassed or maybe even ashamed at how little she was able to give?

When Jesus said she gave more than the other contributors He must have been using a different standard to measure the gift than we use. We usually measure the greatness of a gift by how valuable it is to the receiver. How was Jesus measuring the value of the gifts?

Although this is only the first step in *Flicker Bible study,* look at how much you have pulled from the passage by simply writing down what you see. Bible study is all about what you see. With your two eyes you are fully equipped to surface what God has to say to you.

If you are interested in exploring further the skill of *Seeing* things, there is an Appendix entitled *How Well do You See* on page 239.

Assignment 1

At the end of each chapter is an assignment that w
very long to complete. If you want this material tc
difference in your life, get comfortable and give this assignment a try.

If you get stuck and need more suggestions, more are available in the Appendix titled *Answers*.

Motivation

Take the first step toward uncovering your desire for God
by meditating on the verses on page 20: *1 Peter 2:2, Psalm
42:1-2,* and *Matthew 5:6.* As you do, start thinking about
your own *Desire* for God. Pray that, over time, you will be
able to uncover and strengthen it.

Skill

Take a look at *Mark 6:1-4* on the next page and write out
what you see.

If you get stuck you can check the Appendix titled *Answers*
for some ideas.

Mark 6:1-4

Mark 6:1 Jesus went out from there and came into His hometown; and His disciples followed Him.

Mark 6:2 When the Sabbath came, He began to teach in the synagogue; and the many listeners were astonished, saying, "Where did this man [get] these things, and what is [this] wisdom given to Him, and such miracles as these performed by His hands?

Mark 6:3 "Is not this the carpenter, the son of Mary, and brother of James and Joses and Judas and Simon? Are not His sisters here with us?" And they took offense at Him.

Mark 6:4 Jesus said to them, "A prophet is not without honor except in his hometown and among his [own] relatives and in his [own] household." (NASB)

What do you See in Mark 6:1-4?

"Blessed are those
who hunger and thirst
for righteousness,
for they will be filled."

Matthew 5:6 (NIV1984)

Chapter 2
Uncovering Your Desire

I [N] felt nervous as I stood in the Dallas Theological Seminary bookstore. In a few short weeks I would enter the school as a first year student and I had some serious doubts about my ability to succeed in a program so demanding—especially since my background was engineering and the study of the Bible was basically a liberal arts curriculum.

In engineering, most assignments involved reading a few pages and working out several pages of problems. In DTS, I would be required to read thousands of pages and write several long papers each week.

I knew I needed help with my reading skill so I selected the book *How to Read a Book* from the bookstore. I figured that should take care of things. Then after I took it home and started reading, I noticed the book was over 400 pages long and school started in a few weeks. So I went back to the bookstore and bought the book *How to Read Better and Faster* so I could get through *How to Read a Book*.

The first day of classes arrived and I began the legendary work-load. During the first week I got the assignments for the semester for all my classes and spread them out, as best I could, on a large chart then sat back and shuddered. This was too much work. According to my estimates I would need to study 200 hours each week to keep up.

Denise and I both studied the chart trying to decide what to do. It was clear that God called me to help others study the Bible and DTS had the best program to prepare me for that, but I had to face the looming possibility that I could fail at this.

Then Denise suggested a novel idea. She said this was too much work not to enjoy. "What about just doing what you want to do? If you want to study, then study, if not, then don't. If you want to study a particular subject, then study it, if not, then don't. Let your *Desire* be the guide for what you do and how much you do it. That way, even if you fail, you still get what you wanted from the program."

This sounded like science fiction. I had a natural interest in some of the courses like Greek and Hebrew. But other courses I did not like at all. In one course I needed to explore the oblique process of dating pottery from an archeological site. Plus, my performance in school had only been average up to that point, and I could not see how backing off the push would give me *any* chance of success.

Then something amazing happened. When I consulted what I *wanted* to do, I discovered that a surprising amount of the time I wanted to be responsible.

Encouraged by that, I looked at the courses I did not like, to see if there was anything I wanted to learn from them. Surprisingly, when I took this approach I discovered that it was an interesting puzzle to try and guess the age of a piece of pottery given the little bit of information we have to go on. As I surfaced things I wanted to get from my least favorite courses I was surprised to discover what *I* wanted from the course was not far from what the *professor* wanted me to know.

Once I was in touch with what I wanted to do, creativity came out of nowhere and went to work on the 200 hours per week. I found and interviewed people who were good students and learned what worked for them. I learned how to take better notes in class and how to spend less time studying for tests in content classes. I made sure to give the majority of my time to my favorite courses and figured out ways to do the efficient minimum on classes I liked the least.

After all the dust settled, my schedule was possible—all because it was something I wanted to do.

Make no mistake, following my *Desire* did not guarantee success. In fact, sometimes when there was a lot of pressure and I did not want to study, the idea of following my *Desire* seemed to work against me.

But, in a very surprising way, following my *Desire* put me in *the best place* to succeed because it got me running at peak efficiency, with peak creativity and a positive attitude. It told me when I needed rest and it told me when I could successfully push. The amount of *Discipline* I needed to get through the rough spots felt reasonable since it was in service of accomplishing what I wanted to do.

Your *Desire* is your most effective tool in negotiating a collection of conflicting requirements. There is no more effective arbitrator regardless of your personality. *Desire* helps the hard driving person not burn out. *Desire* helps the free spirit focus without feeling forced.

But *Desire* does not live in a vacuum. Your deepest and truest *Desires* live in the same space as your shallow and passing *Desires* and with things that seem like *Desires* but are not.

How can you distinguish your true *Desires* from the others? Your true *Desires* surface when you minimize the *Desire Squashers* and get a clear fix on what you want the most.

Review Motivation Assignment 1

> *1 Peter 2:2* **Like** *newborn babies,* **crave** *pure spiritual milk, so that by it you may grow up in your salvation (NIV1984)*
>
> *Psalm 42:1-2 As the* **deer pants** *for streams of water, so* **my soul pants for you**, *O God. My soul thirsts for God, for the living God. When can I go and meet with God? (NIV1984)*
>
> *Matthew 5:6 Blessed are those who hunger and thirst for righteousness,* **for they will be filled.** *(NIV1984)*

How did your reflection on these verses go? Did you find them challenging or did they seem unrealistic? These verses describe the goal as we seek to uncover our *Desire* for God (a.k.a. our *"first love"*).

We have more to say about how to do this in the present chapter, but first we need to introduce an influence that works against us and seeks to bury our true *Desires*.

Desire Squasher: Deceitful Desires

As seen in *Chapter 1*, God wants us to uncover our *Desire* for Him and follow it. But as we do, He is careful to warn us about influences that can undermine our *Desire*—let's call these *Desire Squashers*.

We are warned about the first *Desire Squasher* in *Ephesians 4:22-23*.

> *Ephesians 4:22-23 You were taught, with regard to your former way of life, to put off your old self, which is being corrupted by its* **deceitful desires**; *to be made new in the attitude of your minds; (NIV1984)*

What are *Deceitful Desires*? *Deceit* is the misrepresentation of truth, that is, a lie. But how could a *Desire* be a lie?

1. Deceit means

_____

A *Desire* lies when it promises fulfillment but does not deliver. When a *Desire* says that you will be fulfilled if you just go shopping, eating, traveling, gambling, exercising, sleeping, watching TV, looking at pornography, playing sports, buying gadgets, reading romance novels, or burying yourself in work, that is a *Deceitful Desire*. When a *Desire* promises fulfillment but does not deliver, it is *Deceitful*.

2. A *Deceitful Desire* is a *Desire* that promises fulfillment but

_____

When I [D] feel empty or bored, my *Deceitful Desire* of choice is shopping. I think if I just go shopping, I'll feel better. I'll feel some success, because I'll get a cute outfit. I won't torch the budget and will have succeeded at something. I'll be a good shopper with good taste (and I do feel better for awhile). However, this is a *Deceitful Desire* for me because at the end of my life I won't look back and decide my life had meaning because I got a lot of cute outfits.

Following *Deceitful Desires* is like taking emotional anesthesia. It numbs your pain for a while, but like anesthesia, it wears off. If we keep running to the refrigerator, the mall, or the TV for comfort, we never develop the path to God for comfort.

3. If we keep fulfilling *Deceitful Desires*, we never develop

_____ for comfort.

A Grandfather told this Parable of the Wolves to his Grandson:

"There are two wolves living in my heart and they are at war with each other. One is vicious and cruel and the other is wise and kind."

"Grandfather," said the alarmed grandson, "which one will win?"

"The one I feed," said the Grandfather.

We all have well-worn paths to what we think is our help. If our help is *Deceitful*, it is a *Desire Squasher* and will lead us away from finding the help God provides.

But you say, "It can't always be wrong to shop or buy a gadget." You are right. It is often very normal and healthy to do some of these things.

How do you know when a *Desire* is an appropriate comfort and when it is *Deceitful?* The *Desire* becomes *Deceitful* when you rely on it to bring fulfillment or when you consistently rely on it to numb you.

4. A *Desire* becomes *Deceitful* when you rely on it to bring

    _____ or when you rely on it to

    _____

God does not want you to continually escape. He wants you to experience comfort right where you are. God's comfort keeps you in the moment and connects you to Him in the midst of the situation. It is a strange commingling of joy and sadness. Dr. James Dobson says, "God does not give us a detour from problems, but a guided tour through them."

The Old Testament character David was clear that God was the answer for comfort. Look how many times David says "you" in *Psalm 63:1-8.*

> *Psalm 63:1-8 O God, **you** are my God, earnestly I seek **you**; my soul thirsts for **you**, my body longs for **you**, in a dry and weary land where there is no water.*
>
> *I have seen **you** in the sanctuary and beheld **your** power and **your** glory. Because **your** love is better than life, my lips will glorify **you**. I will praise **you** as long as I live, and in **your** name I will lift up my hands. My soul will be satisfied as with the richest of foods; with singing lips my mouth will praise **you**.*
>
> *On my bed I remember **you**; I think of **you** through the watches of the night. Because **you** are my help, I sing in the shadow of **your** wings. My soul clings to **you**; **your** right hand upholds me. (NIV1984)*

David is not turning to *Deceitful Desires* for comfort. He is clear that the answer is not on earth. The earth is a dry and weary land.

David was receiving comfort from God. He said God's love was better than life and satisfied him just like the richest of foods. Visualize biting into the most delicious food you have ever tasted. Can you picture your reaction? Does your head go back with your eyes closed? David is saying his experience with God is like that. His soul clings to God and is comforted.

> 5. Rather than turning to *Deceitful Desires*, David received comfort
>
> _____

As you uncover and begin following your deepest and truest *Desires*, be aware that you will also encounter *Desires* that seem to promise fulfillment but do not deliver. Instead they bury or distract us from the *Desire* God has given us.

The Parable of the Wolf implies that the *Desire* we feed will grow stronger. What *Desire* are you feeding? If we only go to the refrigerator, the car lot, the mall, the TV, or work we could be feeding a *Deceitful Desire* and missing the chance to be comforted by God.

> 6. The *Desire* you feed will
>
> _____

What Do You Want?

But, how can we find our *Desire* for God? I [D] found my *Desire* for God by pondering the following seven questions for a few months.

1. Do I want to know God?

2. How do I want my life to be?

3. Do I want to do His will for my life?

4. Do I want to please God?

5. Do I want to know His heart and what He cares about?

6. Would I prefer my independence over His will and way?

7. It might change my priorities. What do I really want?

Answering these questions for yourself is part of the assignment at the end of this chapter. Be honest as you answer them. See where you hesitate. Notice your reactions. This is like taking your spiritual temperature.

You don't have to tell anyone which questions made you uncomfortable. Although if you did, you would find you are not alone, and that is always encouraging for both people.

Being honest with yourself will enable you to see where you are hesitating. Do you have trouble with the questions that encourage you to know God and please Him? Or is your hesitation more centered around giving up your independence in exchange for His guidance? Are you worried that He will ruin your life if you give it to Him?

Noticing where you hesitate gives you valuable information. If your Christian walk sputters unevenly along, knowing where you might be stuck will help you know where to put your effort to smooth things out.

7. Answering honestly helps you see where you are

_____

If you don't face your hesitations squarely, you may wonder why you are always stepping on the gas then putting on the brake in your walk with Christ.

Ultimately, facing our hesitations squarely and addressing them, gives us the ability to put our foot on the gas and keep it there. God has given His children a *Desire* for Him. Our job is to nurture that *Desire* so it grows.

8. Facing your hesitations helps you know where to place your

_____

Review Skill Assignment 1

Mark 6:1 Jesus went out from there and came into His hometown; and His disciples followed Him.

Mark 6:2 When the Sabbath came, He began to teach in the synagogue; and the many listeners were astonished, saying, "Where did this man [get] these things, and what is [this] wisdom given to Him, and such miracles as these performed by His hands?

Mark 6:3 "Is not this the carpenter, the son of Mary, and brother of James and Joses and Judas and Simon? Are not His sisters here with us?" And they took offense at Him.

Mark 6:4 Jesus said to them, "A prophet is not without honor except in his hometown and among his [own] relatives and in his [own] household." (NASB)

Compare what you *Saw* in these verses with the *Answers* in the Appendix. It is perfectly OK to *See* different things. Just get a sense for what *kind* of things we want you to *See*.

Flicker Bible Study

The *Skill* section in *Chapter 1* introduced the first and most important step in *Flicker Bible Study—Learning to See*. In this *Skill* section we will cover all four steps in *Flicker Bible Study*.

The names of the four steps begin with the letters *F L C and R—Facts, Lessons, Challenges, and Responses.* Pronouncing these letters (FLCR) as *"flicker"* might help you remember the steps more easily.

Don't be worried if the steps do not make perfect sense at first. Give it some time. Learning any skill takes practice: Tying your shoes, riding a bike, driving a car, baking a cake, or knitting all take practice.

Let's first begin by reviewing the first step—*Learning to See*.

Facts

The first step, which we called *Learning to See* in *Chapter 1*, is also called gathering the *Facts* (the *F* in *FLCR*). This is the step where you simply list what you *See*—these are the *Facts* of the passage. It is OK to use the same words the passage uses when you write out the *Facts*. You are just writing short phrases that identify what you are *Seeing*.

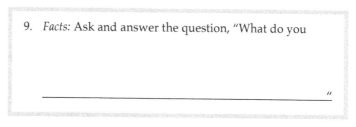

9. *Facts:* Ask and answer the question, "What do you

_____ "

At this point it is a mistake to conclude that you *understand* the passage. It is also a mistake to conclude that you do *not understand* the passage. Rather, withhold judgement and continue writing down what you *See*.

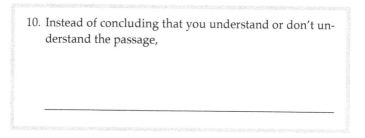

10. Instead of concluding that you understand or don't understand the passage,

_____

Frequently something will catch your attention that you clearly do not understand. Resist the temptation to spend all your time trying to figure it out. Rather, it is much better to focus on what you *can See* and you will be surprised how many of the other things get cleared up along the way.

11. Write down what you *can*

_____

Sometimes you may look at a passage and draw a total blank. If that should happen, ask yourself the *Who, What, Where, When, Why,* questions about the passage. "*Who* is the passage talking about?" "*Where* are they?" "*Why* are they doing this?" "*When* do these events occur?"

If questions occur to you as you are studying the passage, write them in the *Facts* panel along with the other *Facts* you *See.* We will address answering your questions later.

12. *An example Fact:* In *Genesis 12* when God told Abraham to go but He did not tell him where to go, we can *See* the *Fact* that

_____

Lessons

After you identify the *Facts,* the next step is to find the *Lessons* (the *L* in *FLCR*) that can be learned from the *Facts.* Ask yourself, "What can I learn from this passage?" Is there a command to obey, a warning to heed, a promise to hold on to, a comfort to enjoy, or an action that sheds light on God's personality and values? If so, write it down in the form of a principle and that is a *Lesson.*

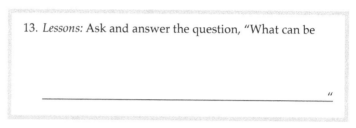

13. *Lessons:* Ask and answer the question, "What can be

_____ "

If you have difficulty finding a *Lesson,* sometimes it is helpful to ask yourself what stands out to you or what you find unusual in the passage. Then figure out a way to say what is unusual about it and see if you can learn from that. If so, write it out in the form of a principle and you have found a *Lesson.*

14. To find a *Lesson* ask yourself what in the passage is the most

    _____

15. Then figure out how to express it and see if you can

    _____

16. *An example Lesson:* In *Genesis 12* when we saw that God did not tell Abraham where to go, we could *Learn* that

    _____

Challenges

The next step is to turn each *Lesson* into a question that *Challenges* (the C in *FLCR*) your life. If you identified two *Lessons*, you should usually come up with two *Challenges*.

In this step you are asking yourself how your life squares with each of the *Lessons* you identified. The purpose of these *Challenges* is *not* to evoke guilt. The purpose is to identify and explore potential ways the truth of the passage touches your life.

It is helpful to begin your *Challenges* with words like this:

- "Am I willing to…" -or-
- "Do I believe that…" -or-
- "Do I agree that…" -or-
- "Do I realize…" -or-
- "Do I value…"

17. *Challenges:* Ask and answer the question, "Where does it touch

_____ "

18. You should have as many *Challenges* as you have

_____

19. *An example Challenge:* In *Genesis 12* when we *Learned* that sometimes God asks us to take action before we have all the necessary information, we could turn that into the question:

_____

Responses

In the last step of *Flicker Bible Study,* sit back and consider what you have surfaced and how it touches your life and listen for what God might be saying to you. God does not always have something to say, but He often does. Listen for Him to speak through His word.

Write out your *Response* (the *R* in *FLCR*) to what God is saying to you. This usually takes the form of a two or three sentence prayer back to God.

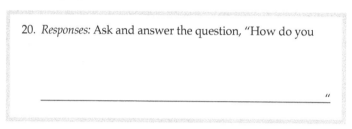

20. *Responses:* Ask and answer the question, "How do you

_____ "

Don't be overly ambitious in your *Response.* Be honest. Don't promise the moon when you know you won't be able to deliver it. This is not a sprint, it is a walk. Ask for help in making the *Lessons* and *Challenges* part of your life. If God is asking you to do something you don't want to do, don't be afraid to *Respond* by asking Him to help you *want* what He *wants.*

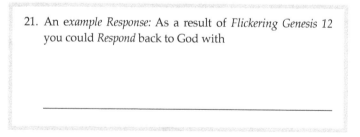

21. An e*xample Response:* As a result of *Flickering Genesis 12* you could *Respond* back to God with

_____

Flicker Practice

Give *Flicker Bible Study* a try! *Flicker* the three short verses on the following pages. Write your answers in the provided *FLCR* panels.

If you get stuck you can check the Appendix titled *Answers* for some ideas.

John 11:35   Jesus wept.
(NASB)

Lessons

Challenges

Responses

Psalm 34:19

Facts

Psalm 34:19 Many are the afflictions of the righteous, But the LORD delivers him out of them all. (NASB)

Lessons

Challenges

Responses

Psalm 19:1 The heavens are telling of the glory of God; And their expanse is declaring the work of His hands. (NASB)

Lessons

Challenges

Responses

About the Flicker Practice

At first it is hard to believe that *John 11:35* is long enough to get anything valuable, but it is.

Remember when you are looking for *Facts*, you are not making anything out of the verse. You are just stating plain things that you see in the verse, e.g. "It is talking about Jesus" or "God's people have many afflictions." You are not really understanding the verse. If you have trouble coming up with *Facts*, you are probably thinking too hard about it. You are just looking at it and writing down things you *See*.

When you are looking for *Lessons*, you are standing back a little bit and identifying what you find unusual about the verse. The unusual part usually has some kind of *Lesson* in it, like "Jesus has emotions" or "I can learn how immense and beautiful God is by looking at the sky."

Remember that *Challenges* are not new things. They just restate the *Lessons* as a question, e.g. "Am I willing to talk to God like He has emotions?" or "When I see a beautiful sunset am I willing to pause and take in what God is telling me about Himself?"

Assignment 2

Motivation

Get quiet each day for several days and answer these questions for yourself each time:

1. Do I want to know God?

2. How do I want my life to be?

3. Do I want to do His will for my life?

4. Do I want to please God?

5. Do I want to know His heart and what He cares about?

6. Would I prefer my independence over His will and way?

7. It might change my priorities. What do I really want?

You are taking your spiritual temperature so be honest when answering these questions. See where you hesitate. If you are honest about where you put on the brakes, then you can do something about it. If you don't face your hesitations squarely, you may wonder why you are always stepping on the gas then putting on the brake in your walk with the Lord.

Skill

Flicker Hebrews 11:8-11. Write out the *Facts, Lessons, Challenges,* and *Responses* in the *FLCR* panels provided on the next couple of pages.

If you get stuck you can check the Appendix titled *Answers* for some ideas.

Hebrews 11:8 By faith Abraham, when he was called, obeyed by going out to a place which he was to receive for an inheritance; and he went out, not knowing where he was going.

Hebrews 11:9 By faith he lived as an alien in the land of promise, as in a foreign [land,] dwelling in tents with Isaac and Jacob, fellow heirs of the same promise;

Hebrews 11:10 for he was looking for the city which has foundations, whose architect and builder is God.

Hebrews 11:11 By faith even Sarah herself received ability to conceive, even beyond the proper time of life, since she considered Him faithful who had promised. (NASB)

Lessons

Challenges

Responses

"For as he thinks
within himself,
so is he."

Prov 23:7a (NASB)

Chapter 3
Renewing Your Mind

As I [N] dove into the pool, I remember being nervous about jumping into the water with these monsters. It was the beginning of my second year of High School and this was my first varsity water polo game.

I had watched the varsity play the previous year while I was on the junior team and marveled at how fast and powerful they were. But after diving in and taking my position in the game, I was amazed how big they were. As the game progressed I had trouble keeping up with my man and was getting pushed around the pool.

Then at half-time, the coach pulled me aside and said, "You are just as big and fast as anyone out there. Now get back in there and don't let anyone get past you." I remember looking at the other players, then looking at myself and being surprised that my coach might be right.

Between my first and second year of High School, I had a dramatic growth spurt in which I gained 20 pounds and several inches of height. My second year sprint times were greatly improved and I had much more overall strength. But I had not updated my thinking.

After half-time I took the coach's advice and, to my surprise, I discovered that I *was* just as fast and just as powerful as anyone out there. For the rest of the game, no one got past me.

What was different in the second half? Had I suddenly become stronger and faster? No, the only thing that changed was my thinking.

The battle is won or lost in your mind.

Review Motivation Assignment 2

What do you want?

1. Do I want to know God?

2. How do I want my life to be?

3. Do I want to do His will for my life?

4. Do I want to please God?

5. Do I want to know His heart and what He cares about?

6. Would I prefer my independence over His will and way?

7. It might change my priorities. What do I really want?

When you think about the questions in this assignment, notice where do you hesitate. The question(s) you hesitate on give you a clue what might be holding down your *Desire* for God. It is possible that some experiences you had in your *Family Of Origin* may be contaminating your *Desire* for Him.

For example, if you hesitate on questions 1 or 6, it may point to an issue of control. If you were physically or emotionally abused by someone in power when you were growing up you might be left worrying that God will abuse His power over you. You might worry that God will ask you to do humiliating things, or suffer, or do things you will hate. What you might not realize, is that while you have been in charge of your life, you have been humiliated, have suffered, and have done things you hated. The difference is, if you hand control of your life over to God, you might suffer but He offers a guarantee that everything will work out to those who love and follow Him *(Rom 8:28)*. Can you make that guarantee of your own leadership?

If you worry about giving control over to God, remember the abuse you suffered happened because of the sinful lack of character in the one who abused you. But God has no sin. You can trust Him. He is love.

The reason there is sin in the world, with its abuse, is God gave us a choice to love and obey Him or be independent from Him. Don't be one of the people that chooses independence from Him. Ignorance is not bliss. Avoiding God so you don't know what He wants is foolish and guarantees heartache.

Embrace God and entrust the control of your life to Him. He has perfect character and will not abuse the power you give Him.

How We Think Effects How We feel

Even if we are not aware of it, we are always thinking. And our thoughts effect us in profound ways. You may be surprised to hear that our thoughts move our feelings which also means our thoughts move our *Desire* for God. Consider the following examples.

Elevator example

Let us suppose a group of people are trapped in an elevator. You would think they would leave the elevator having a similar feeling since they all experienced the same crisis. But that is not how it works.

About a fourth of the people will leave the elevator angry. The whole time they are trapped they are thinking about how they have been inconvenienced. They worry about being late for an appointment and they want to know why the building doesn't maintain their elevators properly.

A fourth will leave the elevator anxious. The whole time they are trapped they are thinking about the safety issues. What if the cable breaks and they plunge down to the basement or what if they run out of oxygen? They rehearse in their mind all of the dangers and so they become anxious.

A fourth will leave excited. While they are trapped, they are planning who they will call to tell about the man who was freaking out or the lady who was so mad. For them, the experience is material to entertain their friends.

The last fourth don't give it much thought. They just wait patiently. They aren't thinking about the inconvenience or safety issues and they don't even mention it to anyone. It is just not that important. They leave the elevator unaffected.

All of these people were trapped on an elevator. But what they were thinking about determined how they ended up feeling.

Job example

Now consider how you would feel if you lost your job.

If you tell yourself, "They have no right to fire me," you will be angry. If you say "I am such a loser, I can't do anything right," you will feel sad.

But if you say, "Well, this isn't the time I would have chosen, but I have been wanting to try something else and now I can," you will feel nervous, but excited for the chance for change.

It is likely that you will cycle through all these thoughts and that is why you feel like a mess—cycling through anger, sadness, excitement, and fear.

Example of Fred

For the final example, let's say we go to a party and I introduce you to Fred. As Fred talks to you, he looks over your shoulder and across the room. At that point, your feelings will be determined by how you interpret his behavior.

If you say to yourself, "Fred is so rude," you will be irritated. If you say, "I bore everyone," you will feel sad. If you say, "Fred seems socially awkward, I wonder if he is shy," you will probably feel some compassion for his discomfort.

People who are continually angry, tend to interpret the events around them as personal insults. Those who are determined to be depressed, see the events around them as evidence of their failure. Neither tune in to the possibility that Fred might be rude or shy due to his own pain.

A Test of Thinking

Victor Frankl was held in the Aushewitz prison camp but he kept his spirits up by realizing his captors could take his family and his life, but they couldn't take away his hope to find meaning even in tragic situations.

After Jesus died on the cross, the disciples had a test of their thinking. When they found Jesus' body missing from the tomb, they had a choice. Some chose to interpret Jesus's missing body as a disaster, but in *John 20:8-9* John chose to believe.

> *John 20:8-9 Finally the other disciple, who had reached the tomb first, also went inside. He saw and **believed**. (They still did not understand from Scripture that Jesus had to rise from the dead.) (NIV1984)*

What miracle in your life are you thinking is a disaster? Jesus' death on the cross looked like a huge disaster. Jesus came to be the king of the Israelites but they killed him. It looked like a failure. Looks can be deceiving. What looked like a failure was actually the biggest victory in the history of mankind.

In each of these examples, the person's feelings depended on what they were thinking. But you may say, "I don't know what I am thinking during the day." Yes, that is often the case.

But, there are a few times during the day when most of us tune in to what we are thinking. One is when the alarm clock goes off. We debate the pros and cons of getting up on time. Another time is the great "should I have one more cookie" debate. We tune in for that too.

1. One time we tune in to what we are thinking is when

    _____

    Or when debating if we should have another

    _____

It is possible to tune in to what we are thinking at other times as well. If you want to change your heart and soul, change comes through your mind. That is why the Bible is in written form.

How We Think Effects How We Grow

Our thoughts spiritually transform us. The Bible describes spiritual change as beginning in our mind.

2. Our thoughts spiritually _____

_____

Before we accepted the forgiveness of sins, *Ephesians 2:3* indicates we were following the *thoughts* of our sinful nature.

> *Ephesians 2:3 All of us also lived among them at one time, gratifying the cravings of our sinful nature and following its desires and **thoughts**... (NIV1984)*

3. Before salvation, our thoughts led us _____

_____

After we accepted the forgiveness of sins, our continuing *Transformation* comes from a renewed *mind*. according to *Romans 12:2*.

> *Romans 12:2 Do not conform any longer to the pattern of this world, but be transformed by the **renewing of your mind**. Then you will be able to test and approve what God's will is—his good, pleasing and perfect will. (NIV1984)*

4. After salvation, our thoughts

_____

In both situations our spiritual direction is a result of what we are thinking about. God's design for change begins in our *minds (Philippians 2:5)*.

> *Philippians 2:5 Let this **mind** be in you, which was also in Christ Jesus: (KJV)*

God is calling for a mind transplant. He did not say "Let this heart be in you" because hearts are broken at times. He wants our minds so we can be steadfast. It is very clear. We are not transformed by obedience. God says let His Word renew your mind, then you will approve His will and likely do it. *(Romans 12:2)*

5. God is calling for a

_____

How does our mind transform us to be more like God? By thinking about things from God's point of view. What kind of things should we be thinking about? The Bible gives us an excellent starting place in *Philippians 4:8.*

> *Philippians 4:8 Finally, brothers, whatever is true, whatever is noble, whatever is right, whatever is pure, whatever is lovely, whatever is admirable—if anything is excellent or praiseworthy—**think about** such things. (NIV1984)*

6. We are transformed by thinking about things

_____

If your friend says "Come on, lets watch this movie where the whole family gets hacked to pieces. It's a true story and we need to know what goes on." Would this fit the *Philippians 4:8* test? It might be true but it doesn't fit the noble, pure, or lovely criteria.

Does that mean we are to just blow sunshine around all the time and not be in reality? No, this verse says to think on things that are "true." So stay in reality. But shift to the way God sees it. There is hope in God's reality.

The Bible presents our thoughts as the battle ground where all is won or lost. Paul describes his strategy for guiding what he thinks about in *2 Corinthians 10:5.*

> *2 Corinthians 10:5 We demolish arguments and every pretension that sets itself up against the knowledge of God, and we **take captive every thought** to make it obedient to Christ. (NIV1984)*

When I [D] first read this verse it seemed overwhelming. How can a person take captive *every* thought?

Then I realized this is telling us what to do with renegade thoughts that argue against the knowledge of God. A renegade thought is a thought like, "That isn't fair," "that was harsh," or "that was wrong." If you find yourself beginning to judge God, you are to take *that* thought captive. You make that thought obedient to Christ. You refuse to judge God when you don't have all the information. It is a test.

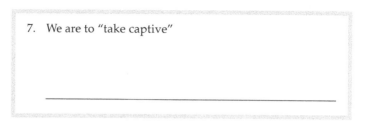

7. We are to "take captive"

_____

What Do You Want?

The strategy we recommend for uncovering the *Desire* God gave you for Him has two parts.

First, it is helpful to answer and ponder these seven questions. This helps you make a realistic appraisal of the current strength of your desire.

1. Do I want to know God?

2. How do I want my life to be?

3. Do I want to do His will for my life?

4. Do I want to please God?

5. Do I want to know His heart and what He cares about?

6. Would I prefer my independence over His will and way?

7. It might change my priorities. What do I really want?

Second, it helps to pray the following three passages back to God. These passages help you grasp the graciousness God has shown to you and respond in kind. Taken together this strategy helps you gently nudge your *Desire* forward.

In the first passage, *Ephesians 3:16-19*, Paul asks God to give the Christians in Ephesus power so they are able to grasp God's love for them.

> *Ephesians 3:16-19 I pray that out of his glorious riches he may strengthen you with power through his Spirit in*

your inner being, so that Christ may dwell in your hearts through faith.

And I pray that you, being rooted and established in love, **may have power,** *together with all the saints,* **to grasp how wide and long and high and deep is the love of Christ,** *and to know this love that surpasses knowledge— that you may be filled to the measure of all the fullness of God. (NIV1984)*

This is something we can also pray for. Here is the same verse arranged as your prayer to God.

"Father I pray that out of Your glorious riches You would strengthen me with power through Your Spirit in my inner being, so that Christ may dwell in my heart through faith.

And I pray that You would root and establish me in this love, so that I may have the power to grasp how wide and long and high and deep is Your love for me, and to know Your love which surpasses knowledge— that I may be filled to the measure of all Your fullness.

Take your time. Ask God to help you. Come back to this verse over and over asking for help and watching for God to help you grasp His love.

The second passage, *Mark 12:30-31,* helps us respond to His love as we begin to understand it.

Mark 12:30-31 "'**Love the Lord your God** *with all your* **heart** *and with all your* **soul** *and with all your* **mind** *and with all your* **strength.**' *The second is this: 'Love your neighbor as yourself.' There is no commandment greater than these.*"

First notice that it says you are to love your neighbor as you love yourself. Raise your hand if you love yourself perfectly. No one loves themselves perfectly. The idea is to do the best you can. Those who are aware how much God loves and forgives them, will be better at loving and forgiving their neighbor. The ultimate goal is to love and forgive the way God does.

Next, notice the dimensions of our response. We are to love God with our mind, strength, heart, and soul. What does that look like?

How do we love God with our mind? Loving God with our mind means that we think the way God wants us to think. How do we interpret what goes on in our life? Do we value the things God values? Do we think about things the way God thinks about them?

It also says to love God with our strength. What does strength imply? Our strength enables our actions and by them our behavior. We should love God by the way we behave.

How do we love God with our heart? The heart is the seat of our feelings. Are our emotions ruled by faith and trust, or by hatred and bitterness, for example.

How do we love God with our soul? The Bible uses heart and soul interchangeably at times. But, the soul stands for the living being. *"God breathed into his nostrils the breath of life and man became a living soul." (Genesis 2:7 KJV)* The soul is what leaves the body at death and goes to be with God. It is who we are apart from our body.

It is helpful to pray this passage back to God and ask Him to help move us in this direction. Here is the passage arranged as a prayer to God.

> "Father I pray that You will help me to love You with all my heart and with all my soul and with all my mind and with all my strength, and help me to love my neighbor as myself because this is what You want most for me."

The third passage, *Luke 18:13b,* helps to round out our perspective. It is already arranged as a prayer to God, so you can pray it directly to God.

Luke 18:13b 'God, have mercy on me, a sinner.' (NIV1984)

This is helpful in a couple of ways. It grounds you if you are proud because you may be thinking you love God more than you actually do. It also gives hope to the weary and unsure person because they focus too intently on how short their love falls.

Praying these three passages back to God and pondering the seven questions will help you uncover the *Desire* God has given you for Him. Don't rush it. Keep coming back to these questions and passages from time to time. The process of restoring your *Desire* may take some time, but it gets the horse back in front of the cart and empowers all of your Time with God.

Desire Squasher: Futile Thinking

If our thinking effects us in profound ways, it only stands to reason that certain kinds of thinking can effect us in negative ways. In *Ephesians 4:17* God cautions us to avoid *Futile Thinking.*

> *Ephesians 4:17 So I tell you this, and insist on it in the Lord, that you must no longer live as the Gentiles do, in the **futility of their thinking**. (NIV1984)*

8. God cautions us to avoid

_____

What is *Futile Thinking?* The word *Futile* implies that something is useless, vain, or that it leads nowhere. It is thinking that does not bear fruit. *Futile Thoughts* are *Thoughts* that lead you nowhere like "He who dies with the most toys wins," or "what happens in Las Vegas stays in Las Vegas."

9. *Futile Thoughts* lead you

_____

Futile Thinking and *Deceitful Desires* (cf. page 34) are both *Desire Squashers*. Rather than strengthening your walk with God, they lead away from God. They focus your attention on substitutes for God that either promise help without delivering it or get you to espouse agreement with nonsensical ideas.

As you ponder the seven questions in the assignment it is important to notice places where you hesitate. Because those may be places where a *Desire Squasher* is at work.

For example, if you hesitate on question three, "Do I want to do His will for my life," you might worry that God's will may interfere with a futile goal like wanting to die "with the most toys." Or, if you hesitate on question one, "Do I want to know God," you may worry that knowing God will interfere with some television watching—which could be a *Deceitful Desire* in that it promises rest and refreshment and often ends up fatiguing you.

As you continue pondering the seven questions, notice where you hesitate. Hesitations point you to what may be holding you back so you can do something about it.

Review Skill Assignment 2

Hebrews 11:8 By faith Abraham, when he was called, obeyed by going out to a place which he was to receive for an inheritance; and he went out, not knowing where he was going.

Hebrews 11:9 By faith he lived as an alien in the land of promise, as in a foreign [land,] dwelling in tents with Isaac and Jacob, fellow heirs of the same promise;

Hebrews 11:10 for he was looking for the city which has foundations, whose architect and builder is God.

Hebrews 11:11 By faith even Sarah herself received ability to conceive, even beyond the proper time of life, since she considered Him faithful who had promised. (NASB)

As you can see in the Appendix titled *Answers* there are several things that can be *Learned* in this passage. But I [N] would like to pick out just one.

What did you make out of the fact that Abraham lived as an alien in the land he had been promised? Why didn't God just give Abraham the land? While there are a few possible answers for that, I am more concerned that you are able to *Learn* from a passage that you do not understand 100% of everything it contains.

Though we don't know why he had to live as an alien, he still did and that is an unusual part of this passage. What is unusual about it?—that the land will belong to Abraham but for some good reason God did not give it to him yet. What can we learn from this unusual thing?

We know that God values faith above many things. Perhaps we can *Learn* that "Sometimes we have to wait for things God promised" or "The faith we develop by waiting for things God promised, may end up more valuable than the thing we were waiting for" or "Since I don't have all the information I should trust God when I have to wait."

Help with Finding the Lessons

The *Skill* section in the last chapter was probably your first exposure to a *Flicker Bible Study*. Don't be worried if the steps are not completely clear. That is the case for most people right now. Hang in there. When it makes sense you'll be glad you did.

While the first step, gathering the *Facts*, is the most important step, the second step, surfacing the *Lessons*, is the trickiest. It is not always obvious what can be learned from the *Facts* of the passage.

> 10. The trickiest step in *Flickering* a passage is finding the
>
> _____

Video Clip

To help you with the *Skill* of finding the *Lessons* we've prepared a video clip that appeared on YouTube some time back. As you watch this video ask yourself, "Can I find something to learn from this video?" The video can be found on the Internet at this location.

https://youtu.be/7DXKZ4JAZBs

"A pencil
is the crowbar
of the mind."

Dr. Howard Hendricks

11. What can you Learn from the Video Clip?

About the Video Clip

Were you able to find anything your could *Learn* from the Video Clip?

When you are watching an event you can learn several things by viewing the experience from different points of view.

From the point of view of the girls in the audience who may be thinking about their own wedding, you could learn something like, "Being close to the water is nice, but there are all kinds of problems being *this close* to the water."

From the point of view of the groomsmen you might learn something like, "The path you walk in a wedding party can have awkward spots where I might stumble and fall. It might be good to practice any tricky sections."

You *learn Lessons* every day by watching experiences around you and concluding things. Later, if you summarize what you *Learned* to someone else you will probably state what you *Learned* as principles like I did above. That is the same thing you do when you *Flicker* a Bible passage.

Flicker Practice

On the next page you will find a Bible passage. Use the same skills you used while watching the Video Clip and *Flicker* the passage in the provided *FLCR* panels.

If you get stuck you can check the Appendix titled *Answers* for some ideas.

Romans 5:8 | Facts

Romans 5:8 But God demonstrates His own love toward us, in that while we were yet sinners, Christ died for us. (NASB)

Lessons

Challenges

Responses

About the Flicker Practice

There are many parts of this verse that you could find *Lessons* in.

What do you *Learn* from the *Fact* that God demonstrated His love? He didn't have to. He could have just told us He loved, never demonstrated it, and required that we take it by faith.

What do you *Learn* from the *Fact* that He demonstrated His love before we repented? Here are some possibilities, "God knows we can't help sinning" or "Real love is doing something for someone who doesn't deserve it." From our point of view we can *Learn* that "Wow, God really does love us."

What can you *Learn* from the *Fact* that God showed his love by Christ dying for us? Here are some possibilities, "Love requires sacrifice" or "sin requires death" or "Christ's death paid for our sin so we wouldn't have to."

Finally, you can almost always *Learn* something about God from every passage of scripture. For example from this passage, what kind of person does something for someone without demanding that it be earned or deserved? The people I've [N] come across that are given to this kind of thing are kind souls that have a twinkle in their eye and get more out of giving than receiving. ***That*** is what God is like. The next time you pray, do you think you could conceptualize God as having that kind of attitude?

Assignment 3

Motivation

1. Do I want to know God?

2. How do I want my life to be?

3. Do I want to do His will for my life?

4. Do I want to please God?

5. Do I want to know His heart and what He cares about?

6. Would I prefer my independence over His will and way?

7. It might change my priorities. What do I really want?

Continue to ponder these seven questions and the three verses: *Ephesians 3:16-19, Matthew 12:30-31,* and *Luke 18:13.* Ask God to help you grasp and embrace His love.

At the request of people who have taken the course, these questions and verses have also been placed into a convenient reminder format in the Appendix titled *Reminder Card* on page 235.

Skill

Flicker Genesis 12:1-5. Write out the *Facts, Lessons, Challenges,* and *Responses* in the *FLCR* panels provided on the next couple of pages.

Also, read the Appendix that is titled *More Help with Finding the Lessons.* This extends the help provided by the Video Clip in this chapter and identifies approaches that help finding *Lessons* in any Bible passage.

If you get stuck on *Genesis 12:1-5* you can check the Appendix titled *Answers* for some ideas.

Genesis 12:1-5

Facts

Genesis 12:1 Now the Lord said to Abram, "Go forth from your country, And from your relatives And from your father's house, to the land which I will show you;

Genesis 12:2 And I will make you a great nation, And I will bless you, And make your name great; And so you shall be a blessing;

Genesis 12:3 And I will bless those who bless you, And the one who curses you I will curse. And in you all the families of the earth will be blessed."

Genesis 12:4 So Abram went forth as the Lord had spoken to him; and Lot went with him. Now Abram was seventy-five years old when he departed from Haran.

Genesis 12:5 Abram took Sarai his wife and Lot his nephew, and all their possessions which they had accumulated, and the persons which they had acquired in Haran, and they set out for the land of Canaan; thus they came to the land of Canaan. (NASB)

Lessons

Challenges

Responses

"The point of life
is to get to know Jesus
in every situation."

Oswald Chambers

Chapter 4
Independence or Walking Toward God?

I [D] went to a 'secular' school for my Master's of Psychology degree. I think there was only one other Christian in the whole program. I remember raising my hand one day in class and commenting, "We are real big on the idea of boundaries in psychology. We teach our clients that it is OK to tell someone else that 'this' is OK with me, but 'this other thing' is not OK. And I agree that boundaries are important because without them there would be no right or wrong.

"But, I've noticed that psychology doesn't seem to like the idea that God might have boundaries! He has to be the big doormat in the sky. He has to accept whatever we justify in our own minds." Well, you could have heard a pin drop in the room after that.

God does have boundaries. He wrote a whole book about them. They are reasonable and His help is available within them.

Review Motivation Assignment 3

1. Do I want to know God?

2. How do I want my life to be?

3. Do I want to do His will for my life?

4. Do I want to please God?

5. Do I want to know His heart and what He cares about?

6. Would I prefer my independence over His will and way?

7. It might change my priorities. What do I really want?

As you ponder these questions, be sure to notice where you hesitate because that can give you a clue what might be holding your *Desire* for God down.

For example, if you hesitate on question 2, "How do I want my life to be?" you may be thinking you don't have a say in how your life is going to go. Somewhere along the way you may have picked up a child's victim mentality. You may think life happens to you and you can't do anything about it.

That is a child's way of thinking because that is true for children. They don't have power or resources to alter the course of their life. They depend on the adults in their life for their well being.

But, that is not true for adults. Adults have power, they have resources, and they can make decisions that make their situations better. When life happens to adults, they spring into action. They use their resources to reach out and make their situation better. They pray and follow God. Their faith in God's sovereignty comforts them like faith in a good parent's power is comforting for a child.

If you hesitate about question 2 because you worry about life happening to you, step back and take stock of who you are today. Realize as an adult you have power and resources and the ability to make choices that can make your situation a little better.

Another reason some people hesitate on question 2 is if they picked up a passive way of thinking some where along the way. For example, if our parents took care of everything for us, shielding us from the consequences of our poor choices, and we were allowed to passively enjoy the benefits of their work, we can develop what Dr. Frank Minrith calls *super-spiritual passivity*. We think God should handle everything in our life like our parents did and we twist Bible verses into supporting that thinking.

We don't want to say how we want our life to be because then we would be responsible for our life. We want God to be responsible for how it goes. If we want to get married we expect God to deliver the spouse to us without effort on our part. We think it is not just *spiritual* to be passive and wait, we think it is *super-spiritual*—better than everyone else. If we need a job we expect God to put it all together for us.

But unfortunately, this kind of *spiritual passivity* is not only wrong, it causes us to begin resenting God when He refuses to do all we are expecting. God doesn't want us to be passive, He says, *"take My yoke on you" (Matthew 11:29)*. He wants us to pull the weight with Him. We are partners with Him. He is in control, but He wants His children to step out in faith trusting Him to lead. If you are having trouble knowing how you want your life to be (question 2) because you expect God to do everything, consider becoming His partner.

Independence from God

There is a baffling tendency in all of us to turn and run from help. We are so sure we know better. But our actions so often separate us from the help we need.

In fact, this tendency is at the root of all sin. In its essence, sin is not wrong doing. Rather, sin is independence from God. Independent thinking says, "I'm not going to be any-one's disciple," "I'm my own boss," and "I do, what *I* want to do."

1. Sin is

_____

Most of us know non-Christians who behave better than many Christians. Going to heaven is not about behaving better than other people. Otherwise these well-behaved non-Christians would be going to heaven.

The reason non-Christians are not going to heaven is that they reject God's provision of forgiveness. They choose hell when they say, "I am my own boss. I don't need forgiveness." The Christian knows he is dependent on God's mercy and needs forgiveness.

2. Believers are dependent on

_____

God offers forgiveness and unconditional love within certain boundaries. He made the way. But independence from Him foils His efforts.

God's Help

In the last days of His ministry on earth, Jesus gave an object lesson during a meal. He wanted His disciples to understand what was going to happen over the next few days and He wanted to describe how God provides His help. The object lesson is described in *Mark 14:22ff.*

> *Mark 14:22 And as they did eat, Jesus **took** bread, and **blessed**, and **brake** it, and **gave** to them, and said, Take, eat: this is my body. (KJV)*

As you may recognize, this was the last supper they had together. In the object lesson…

- Jesus took the bread,
- Jesus blessed the bread,
- Jesus broke the bread, and
- Jesus gave the bread.

3. Jesus…

_____ the bread

_____ the bread

_____ the bread

_____ the bread

This pattern describes the way God worked with Jesus' life in that…

- God took Jesus,
- God blessed Jesus,
- God broke Jesus, and
- God gave Jesus.

This is the way God provides His help to us—He broke Jesus by placing our sin upon Him and gave Jesus over to receive the punishment that we deserve.

This is also the way God works in our life and through our life to help others...

- God takes us,
- God blesses us,
- God breaks us, and
- God gives us.

We like the "taking us" part and the "blessing us" part. But we cry foul at the "breaking us" part. *"He that loveth his life shall lose it." (John 12:25 KJV)* If we clutch at our life and say, "No, this is my life you can't have it," our life stays in our tight fist.

> John 12:24-28 *"I tell you the truth, unless a kernel of wheat falls to the ground and dies, it remains only a single seed. But if it dies, it produces many seeds.* **The man who loves his life will lose it,** *while the man who hates his life in this world will keep it for eternal life. Whoever serves me must follow me; and where I am, my servant also will be. My Father will honor the one who serves me. Now my heart is troubled, and what shall I say? 'Father, save me from this hour'? No, it was for this very reason I came to this hour. Father, glorify your name!" Then a voice came from heaven, "I have glorified it, and will glorify it again." (NIV1984)*

If we are not "broken" like that kernel of wheat falling to the ground and dying, our life remains a single seed, never leaving our clutches, never breaking away, never producing many seeds, and never being given to many.

Jesus wasn't crazy about the "breaking" process either. He said, *"Father let this cup pass from Me" (Matthew 26:39)*. But He was willing to go through it.

I [D] remember watching the movie *Horse Whisperer* several years ago. If you didn't see the movie, it is about a young teenage girl who gets hit by a truck while riding her horse. The horse was badly injured and scared. The veterinarian and those who loved the horse kept trying to approach the horse to help him, but the horse kept bucking and rearing up and fighting the helpers because he was hurt and scared.

As I watched the movie, I realized I was like that horse. We had been going through a difficult time too and I found myself hurt, scared, and bucking around. But, just like the horse, I couldn't get the help I needed if I kept fighting the situation.

When you are struggling, fighting, and bucking, the thing that helps is to stop fighting, accept that you are in a difficult situation, and walk toward the help. Sometimes the help is confiding in a friend. Sometimes it is asking help from a pastor or professional. But it always includes walking toward God for help. When you walk toward God, you are agreeing to put His yoke on, as it says in *Matthew 11:28-30*, so you won't have to carry the whole burden.

> *Matthew 11:28-30 "Come to me, all you who are weary and burdened, and I will give you rest.* **Take my yoke upon you** *and learn from me, for I am gentle and humble in heart, and you will find rest for your souls. For* **my yoke is easy and my burden is light**." *(NIV1984)*

A yoke is a harness that helps two animals distribute the load between them. You will notice when God tells you to put His yoke on, you are still carrying some of the burden. You are in the yoke. But now you have help. You are not supposed to throw your burdens on God and try to forget them. You work as a team with God. Our burdens are not meant to be carried alone.

Jesus walked toward the task before Him. He was not bucking around. He wanted God to be glorified. Being fruitful implies carrying a burden. Picture a beautiful tree full of luscious fruit. It is carrying the burden of fruit it was meant to carry. It can feed and refresh many. But we can't bear fruit until we stop fighting and accept God's yoke.

God can redeem anything we give Him. He *works all things together for good to those who love Him. (Romans 8:28)* This is not a blank check. He is not promising to work all things together for good to those who hate Him and work against Him.

But, for those who love Him, He wants us to give Him our ugliest parts to fix. We have the same kind of willingness that the man in *Mark 3:1-6* had.

> *Mark 3:1-6 Another time he went into the synagogue, and* **a man with a shriveled hand** *was there. Some of them were looking for a reason to accuse Jesus, so they watched him closely to see if he would heal him on the Sabbath. Jesus said to the man with the shriveled hand, "Stand up in front of everyone." Then Jesus asked them, "Which is lawful on the Sabbath: to do good or to do evil, to save life or to kill?" But they remained silent. He looked around at them in anger and, deeply distressed at their stubborn hearts, said to the man, "Stretch out your hand." He stretched it out, and his hand was completely restored. Then the Pharisees went out and began to plot with the Herodians how they might kill Jesus. (NIV1984)*

Can you imagine the man in *Mark 3:1-6* with the shriveled hand, being asked to stand in front of everyone and stretch out his most shameful part? This was a tough, judgemental crowd. But he was willing to do it and God redeemed his hand.

God can redeem whatever we give Him—even if its ugliness is of our own doing. It might take some time, but God can redeem it.

Don't clutch your independence. Be like a kernel of wheat and be willing to die to your own agenda. Walk toward God, by getting to know Him, so His love can compel you and your life can produce a harvest of seeds.

Desire Squasher: Taking Offense

When God's help includes hardship it is very easy to get on the wrong side of things and *Take Offense*.

We have pointed out a couple of *Desire Squashers—Deceitful Desires* and *Futile Thinking*—that can sabotage your *Desire* to know God. This next *Desire Squasher* is described in *Mark 4* and *John 6*.

> *Mark 4:19-20 but the worries of this life, the deceitfulness of wealth and the desires for other things come in and choke the word, making it unfruitful. Others, like seed sown on good soil, hear the word, **accept it**, and produce a crop—thirty, sixty or even a hundred times what was sown. (NIV1984)*

> *John 6:53-56, 60-61, 66 Jesus said to them, "I tell you the truth, unless you eat the flesh of the Son of Man and drink his blood, you have no life in you. Whoever eats my flesh and drinks my blood has eternal life, and I will raise him up at the last day. For my flesh is real food and my blood is real drink. Whoever eats my flesh and drinks my blood remains in me, and I in him."*

> *On hearing it, many of his disciples said, "This is a hard teaching. **Who can accept it?**" Aware that his disciples were grumbling about this, Jesus said to them, "**Does this offend you?**"*

> *From this time many of his disciples turned back and no longer followed him. (NIV1984)*

The third *Desire Squasher* is *Taking Offense*. More people's faith becomes neutralized because they *Take Offense* about something than any other thing.

We are vulnerable for *Taking Offense* because we don't have God's perspective. We don't have all the information. We should withhold judgment and take *that* thought captive.

4. We have mentioned two *Desire Killers* to watch out for.

_____ and

_____

The third *Desire Killer* is

_____

In *John 6* the disciples heard Jesus say they needed to *"eat my flesh and drink my blood"* and went "eww... That sounds like cannibalism." They got on their moral high-horse pretty quickly, deciding they understood Jesus, and they concluded He was wrong. They were quick to *Take Offense.*

Jesus gave them a chance to clear up their misconception. He said, *"Does this offend you?"* But, they were too sure they understood and turned away, never to follow Him again.

We can *Take Offense* too. When evil triumphs and we don't understand what is going on, we can *Take Offense.* When we suffer loss and heartache, we can judge God and turn away. Sometimes we don't even admit that we have *Taken Offense.* We just subtly turn back and gradually leave God. But it is because we *Took Offense.*

The answer to this challenge is not complex but it requires some patience. When we feel tempted to *Take Offense,* we should remember that we don't have all the information.

5. When we feel tempted to *Take Offense* we should remember that we do not have

_____ and we should

_____

Instead of deciding that we see all the issues clearly and quickly judging God, we should remind ourselves of His love, character, and trustworthiness. Then we should take our judgmental thought captive (as described on page 69).

Review Skill Assignment 3

One of the *Skill* assignments was to read the Appendix titled *More Help with Finding the Lessons*. Make sure you get the idea of viewing passages from different points of view. There is another example of that in the *Genesis 12:1-5* assignment below. Also, don't miss the idea that every passage is written by two authors and is written to two different audiences.

The other assignment was to *Flicker Genesis 12:1-5*.

> *Genesis 12:1 Now the Lord said to Abram, "Go forth from your country, And from your relatives And from your father's house, to the land which I will show you;*

> *Genesis 12:2 And I will make you a great nation, And I will bless you, And make your name great; And so you shall be a blessing;*

> *Genesis 12:3 And I will bless those who bless you, And the one who curses you I will curse. And in you all the families of the earth will be blessed."*

> *Genesis 12:4 So Abram went forth as the Lord had spoken to him; and Lot went with him. Now Abram was seventy-five years old when he departed from Haran.*

> *Genesis 12:5 Abram took Sarai his wife and Lot his nephew, and all their possessions which they had accumulated, and the persons which they had acquired in Haran, and they set out for the land of Canaan; thus they came to the land of Canaan. (NASB)*

One *Fact* to notice about this passage is that God told Abram (whose name is latter changed to Abraham) to leave and go but does not tell him where to go. From that we can *Learn* that sometimes God asks us to take action before we have all the necessary information. Turning that into a *Challenge*, "If God wants me to take action about something before I have all the information, would I be willing to take action?"

Did you notice that God told Abram to leave his home town and all things familiar, yet it was ok for him to take all his possessions? Is there something to *Learn* there?

As you looked for unusual things that you might be able to *Learn* from in the passage, doesn't it seem unusual and nice how eager God is to bless Abraham? Most people don't do such great things for someone else and usually only if there is some king of big payoff to make it worthwhile. But we can *Learn* that "God shares His glory and greatness" from the *Fact* that God is going to make Abram's name great. Turning that into a *Challenge*, "Am I willing to wealth and gifts with others to help them succeed?"

In this passage, notice that you can look at it from more than one perspective. We have been looking at it all from Abram's perspective, but we can *Learn* different things from Sarah's perspective. From the *Facts* that "God spoke with Sarah's husband," "God told him to go," and that "He obeyed," we can *Learn* that "Sometimes God's will for a family member will have huge implications on us." Turning that into a *Challenge*, "If God leads or allows a family member to go through experiences that turn our life upside down, are we willing to look for and trust that He has something important for us to learn as well?"

Flicker Practice

Flicker the short verses on the following pages. Write your answers in the provided *FLCR* panels.

If you get stuck you can check the Appendix titled *Answers* for some ideas.

Philippians 2:4

Facts

Philippians 2:4 do not [merely] look out for your own personal interests, but also for the interests of others. (NASB)

Lessons

Challenges

Responses

Psalm 56:3-4   Facts

Psalm 56:3 When I am afraid, I will put my trust in You.

Psalm 56:4 In God, whose word I praise, In God I have put my trust; I shall not be afraid. What can [mere] man do to me? (NASB)

Lessons

Challenges

Responses

About Flicker Practice

It is very easy to jump past the first step of finding the *Facts*. If you think that restating what is in the verse is unnecessary and obvious you would be partially right. Sometimes it feels that way.

But the ability to *See Facts* in a verse is of foundational important. It gives you the ability to go to any verse in the Bible, no matter how hard, and *See Facts* in the verse. You are not totally stuck. You are not totally stumpted.

In fact, when you are in a verse that makes no sense, the way to go forward in your understanding is to keep looking at verse with fresh new eyes and just state what you *See*.

Notice I didn't say finding the *Facts* was fast or easy. But developing the ability of not having to have the answer right away and being willing to continue looking at the verse with fresh eyes gets you past the surface, gives you more information to consider, and gives you time devise more ways to look at it.

If you have listed all the *Facts* you can find and you want to see more, especially in longer passages, you could start looking for structural *Facts*.

- *Comparisons:* are two things being compared?
- *Contrasts:* are two things being contrasted?
- *General to Specific:* do you *See* a progression from general things to specific things?
- *Specific to General:* do you *See* the opposite?
- *Climax:* are the events in the story building to a climax? If so, when does it start building and when does it climax?

Facts may seem meaningless but after all is said and done, the better you are at this, the better you are at Bible study.

Assignment 4

Motivation

1. Do I want to know God?

2. How do I want my life to be?

3. Do I want to do His will for my life?

4. Do I want to please God?

5. Do I want to know His heart and what He cares about?

6. Would I prefer my independence over His will and way?

7. It might change my priorities. What do I really want?

Continue to ponder these seven questions and the three verses: *Ephesians 3:16-19, Matthew 12:30-31*, and *Luke 18:13*. See if you can locate your *Desire* to know God. Ask God to help you grasp and embrace His love.

Skill

Flicker Matthew 18:1-4. Write out the *Facts, Lessons, Challenges*, and *Responses* in the *FLCR* panels provided on the next couple of pages.

If you get stuck you can check the Appendix titled *Answers* for some ideas.

Matthew 18:1 At that time the disciples came to Jesus and said, "Who then is greatest in the kingdom of heaven?"

Matthew 18:2 And He called a child to Himself and set him before them,

Matthew 18:3 and said, "Truly I say to you, unless you are converted and become like children, you will not enter the kingdom of heaven.

Matthew 18:4 "Whoever then humbles himself as this child, he is the greatest in the kingdom of heaven. (NASB)

Lessons

Challenges

Responses

"Faith in God's character
is the heroic effort of life.
Have reckless confidence
in God."

Oswald Chambers

Chapter 5
Removing Thorns

When an elephant is very young, one end of a rope is tied around one of its feet and the other is tied to a stake in the ground. The elephant is not big enough or strong enough to dislodge the stake so, before long, it stops trying.

After the elephant grows up, the stake is no longer needed. All they have to do is tie one end of a rope around the elephant's foot, leaving the other end free, and the elephant will not attempt to wander off. At an early age the elephant learned that it was impossible to walk away when the rope was tied to its foot, so there is no need to try it again.

The experiences you have when you are young and the way you chose to respond to those experiences become a collection of learned patterns that follow you throughout life. They are lessons you have learned and conclusions you have made about yourself and the world around you.

Since these patterns were learned at an early age they have been integrated into your collection of automatic reactions and you seldom, if ever, question your automatic reactions.

In most cases the patterns are helpful. Lessons you learned as a child like "Don't run into a street when a car is coming," "Don't touch a hot stove," "Hard work pays off," and "Honesty is the best policy" provide healthy automatic patterns for adult behavior.

But some patterns you learned were only appropriate when you were a small child in a difficult situation like "Stay clear of dad, he is always in a bad mood," "Make sure you are no trouble to anyone so you don't make mom feel worse," or "My parents don't come through for me so I won't count on people." Even though you don't need these patterns after you grow up, they have been integrated into your collection of automatic reactions and you continue to live by them. These inappropriate patterns can cause you to behave in ways that may not make sense to your current situation.

This can be especially true when you deal with God because we come to Him as our Father. He treats us like family *(Galatians 4:6-7)*, Jesus treats us like family *(Matthew 12:50)*, and our natural response back to God is a family response. That is when our learned *Family of Origin* patterns kick in. Your *Family of Origin* is the family you grew up in. Most of the time, the patterns you respond with are appropriate and make sense to apply toward God.

> 1. Your *Family of Origin* is the family
>
> _____

But when our learned patterns are not appropriate to apply toward God, they become *Family of Origin Issues* and need to be updated.

Review Motivation Assignment 4

1. Do I want to know God?

2. How do I want my life to be?

3. Do I want to do His will for my life?

4. Do I want to please God?

5. Do I want to know His heart and what He cares about?

6. Would I prefer my independence over His will and way?

7. It might change my priorities. What do I really want?

Sometimes our *Family of Origin* experiences can cause us to worry about question 3, "Do I want to do His will for my life? We might worry that if we give God control of our life He might ruin it.

If our parents seldom wanted what was good for us but focused only on what was good for them, it can make it harder to believe God's will would be good for us. We are tempted to doubt God's character because our parents didn't put our well being first. Our parents might have been self-centered and put their needs first and we worry that God might be the same way. He might use us for His purposes that aren't so good for us.

While it might be true that your parents were self-centered and that you got hurt because of it, it does not follow that God's treatment of you will be harmful. He promises to work out things for those who love Him and do His will *(Rom 8:28)*. Have you ever noticed that things tend to work out for those who love and obey God? I would hate to get to heaven and see all that God had planned for me but I was too worried to trust Him.

In fact, He has proven that He puts our needs above His needs when He sent Jesus to die for our sins *(Rom 8:32)*. Are you willing to believe that His will is good for us?

Family of Origin Issues

There are two kinds of experiences in your *Family of Origin* that can hinder your walk with God.

The first is if you trusted a significant adult in your past and then got burned. If that is the background you bring to the Christian life, it may be harder for you to trust God.

Now, some people are hesitant to think about their *Family Of Origin Issues (FOOI pronounced FOO eee)*. They think if they do so, they are being disloyal to their parents. But, if you are willing to face unfinished business that is still affecting you today, you will end up able to love your parents more, not less. You will no longer be a "victim." of your outdated automatic reactions.

Parents are responsible for taking care of their children from birth until 18 years of age. Once you turn 18, *you* are responsible to take over the care of yourself, not your parents.

2. It is your parent's job to meet your needs from birth to

    _____

3. After that, meeting your needs is

    _____

If you are a parent and you unwittingly did something that hurt your child, would you want them to stand before God and say "my parents damaged me a bit so I wasn't able to serve You very much?" Or would you want them to face the problem, take responsibility and fix it so they could be good stewards of the life God has given them?

If you face your unfinished business, you are not being disloyal, you are being responsible. It probably makes sense that *FOOI* can hinder your personal relationships, but it may be surprising to discover that it can also hinder you spiritually? (see *Mark 4:7*).

*Mark 4:7 Other seed fell among **thorns**, which grew up and choked the plants, so that they did not bear grain. (NIV1984)*

I [D] think the "thorns" that choked out the fruitfulness of the plants in *Mark 4:7* could be unfinished business from past *FOOI*. These patterns are automatic and can significantly hinder your ability to give yourself wholeheartedly to our heavenly Father.

Are there issues, related to growing up, that may be choking out your fruitfulness? For instance, if one of your parents was unavailable emotionally, you might be tempted to think God will also be unavailable to you.

The second way you might have experienced *FOOI* is if you encountered unique circumstances like the loss of a parent for example. That is how I [D] experienced *FOOI*. My father died unexpectedly when I was 3 years old. Because of that, I found that total surrender to the Lord was unusually hard. Because of my FOOI I feared something catastrophic might happen. I didn't realize that I was living my adult life from a three year old's mind-set. My three year old mind-set said that life "happens" to you. You have no power or options. It is all "God's sovereignty" and no "man's responsibility." Unlike most adults who take responsibility and make use of their resources, I had a three year old's powerless mind-set. This made me more worried about surrendering to God because I felt powerless to deal with what He might allow.

Family Of Origin Issues can Distort Bible Study

Whatever *FOOI* you may have picked up along the way follows you into every area of your Christian life. *FOOI* can even contaminate how you interpret the Bible.

4. *FOOI* effects how you interpret

_____

For example, when you read *Romans 3:23* you could have one of a few different responses.

> Romans 3:23 *for **all have sinned** and fall short of the glory of God. (NIV1984)*

In a balanced response you might be sobered. You would figure that we all might fall short, but there is some relief in the fact that we are all in the same boat. It would also be a relief to learn that God is not in the boat. He is greater than us.

But a *FOOI* response might say, "God is impossible to please just like my dad (or mom). They were impossible to please. I always fell short of their requirements no matter what I did. God might have paid for my sins, but I am convinced that He is not OK with me."

Be careful not to put your *FOOI* on God. If you could never please a parent, that parent was not OK.

I heard of a teenage boy who could never please his father. The boy was excited when he got straight A's on his report card. He thought to himself, "Now dad will have to be pleased." But when he showed the report card to his father, his father slammed his fist onto the table and said, "I knew you could get all A's. You have been holding out on me. Why haven't you been doing this all along?"

If you had a parent who could never be pleased, there was something wrong in their life. Don't put your parent's face on God and you will get much more from your Bible study.

5. God does not have your parent's

_____

Get to Know God

The antidote for much of *FOOI* is to get to know God. He is your new parent and is very reasonable and kind. The better you know Him and replace old patterns with patterns consistent with what God is truely like, the less your *FOOI* will contaminate your present life.

6. The antidote for much of *FOOI* is to

_____

One helpful way to get to know God is to start compiling a list that describes what God is like. As you study a passage and learn a new trait of God's character, add it to your list and begin to get a profile of your new parent. Here are some traits to get you started.

- God is slow to anger
  (Exodus 34:6)

- God's mercies are new every morning
  (Lamentations 3:23)

- God is rich in kindness
  (Exodus 34:6)

- God is Holy
  (1 Samuel 2:2, Isaiah 6:3)

- God always does what is right
  (Genesis 18:25)

- God is perfect
  (Deuteronomy 32:4)

- God is not needy
  (Acts 17:25)

- God is love
  (1 John 4:8)

- God never sins when He is angry
  (Deuteronomy 32:4)

- God made a way for me to be forgiven
  (John 3:16)

- God has my best interest in mind
  (Luke 11:13)

Identify How God Differs From Your Parents

As you get a profile of what God is like, pay particular attention to how He differs from your parents. You might be surprised to learn what "delights" God in *Jeremiah 9:24*.

> *Jeremiah 9:24* *"Boast in this... that he understands and* **knows Me***, that I am the Lord who exercises kindness, justice, and righteousness on earth, for in these I delight." (NIV1984)*

In *Jeremiah 9:24* God asserts that He wants us to understand and know the real Him. He doesn't want us to mistake Him for a flawed composite of our parents.

7. God wants us to know Him, not a flawed composite

_____

If you ask a seven year old what God is like, he or she will describe their dad or their most significant parent. That is normal and good. God has designed the family to teach children about Him.

It is OK for a seven year old to think God is like his parents but it may not be so appropriate for an adult to think God is like his earthly parents. For example, God doesn't have a hair trigger temper or a mean streak, or whatever flaw may have characterized your parents.

If you find yourself having trouble trusting God, see if your difficulty might be connected to *FOOI*. Get quiet and notice more carefully what feeling you are having about God—fear, anger, sadness, or something else. See if your feeling seems "old" and well practiced. Do you remember frequently feeling like this in response to a parent?

As you think about your response, start thinking about how God differs from your parents. If you are worried that God is explosive because you had an explosive dad, start listing how God is different. For example He is slow to anger, His mercies are new every morning, He made the way for you to be forgiven.

Sometimes we have learned responses to life situations from the past. For example, if things are going well yet you have trouble enjoying it, that could be a learned response. Who did you learn it from?

Maybe mom was volatile and moody and you couldn't trust her "good mood" because you knew her good mood could turn on a dime and you needed to be ready to duck. That is a learned response and it can easily contaminate your relationship with God.

You are most vulnerable to these kind of reactions when God is leading you through a time of waiting. If you are not getting what you want, you will want to know why. If you can't see a reason, you will fill in the reason from what is familiar—from *FOOI*.

When you are trying to trust God, but feel troubled because of *FOOI*, it helps to...

- Get quiet and pray for wisdom

- Write down what your response to God is—fear, sadness, anger,...?

- Look for the source of your response—is it learned from a parent, is it similar to how you responded to a parent?

- Write down how God differs from your parent concerning this issue.

These steps help you surface the *FOOI* pattern that is distracting you and it helps you learn something about God that can give you relief from the difficult life experience.

If you had difficult parents, *Psalm 27:10* says that God is kind and will receive you. God is not like our flawed parents. He must get weary of the accusation.

> *Psalm 27:10 Though my father and mother forsake me, **the Lord will receive me**. (NIV1984)*

If you find yourself struggling with the idea of authority, for example, and suspect that *FOOI* may be involved, consider this: Ice cream is delicious unless it is jammed down your throat. But ice cream is still delicious. The problem is not with the ice cream but with the manner in which it is served.

If you had difficult parents and they jammed "authority" down your throat, the problem is not with authority, but with how it was served. God won't jam it down your throat. He is kind.

Start tuning in to your reactions as you study the Bible and serve God. When you detect a *FOOI* pattern at work, surface what is going on and distinguish how God differs from the significant authorities of the past.

Review Skill Assignment 4

> *Matthew 18:1 At that time the disciples came to Jesus and said, "Who then is greatest in the kingdom of heaven?"*
>
> *Matthew 18:2 And He called a child to Himself and set him before them,*
>
> *Matthew 18:3 and said, "Truly I say to you, unless you are converted and become like children, you will not enter the kingdom of heaven.*
>
> *Matthew 18:4 "Whoever then humbles himself as this child, he is the greatest in the kingdom of heaven. (NASB)*

What I [N] find most unusual about this passage is how Jesus answers the question about *"who is greatest"* with an example that seems the opposite of a great person—a child. There must be qualities that a child has in abundance that help us see what God values.

From *verse 4* we can *Learn* that "God values those who are humble." Since Jesus sets up such a deliberate analogy you could extend the description and *Learn* from that. Children are also simple, they believe easily, and are tender and open to learn. So you could *Learn* that "God values people that simplify their thinking, that easily believe Him, and that are tender and open to learn from Him." Turning those *Lessons* into *Challenges*, "Am I willing to simplify my thinking and be open to believe God?"

Flicker Practice

Flicker the short verses on the following pages. Write your answers in the provided *FLCR* panels.

John 6:35

Facts

John 6:35 Jesus said to them, "I am the bread of life; he who comes to Me will not hunger, and he who believes in Me will never thirst. (NASB)

www.WaveStudyBible.com

Chapter 5

Lessons

Challenges

Responses

Psalm 139:14

Facts

Psalm 139:14   I will give thanks to You, for I am fearfully and wonderfully made; Wonderful are Your works, And my soul knows it very well. (NASB)

Lessons

Challenges

Responses

About Flicker Practice

As you *Flicker* passages remember when you construct your *Challenges*, it is best to start your *Challenge* with one of these phrases. The first phrase is the most helpful.

- "Am I willing to..." -or-
- "Do I believe that..." -or-
- "Do I agree that..." -or-
- "Do I realize..." -or-
- "Do I value..."

Here are several *Lesson / Challenge* pairs to help you get the idea how to contruct *Challenges* from *Lessons.*

Lesson:	God wants us to trust Him for our well being.
Challenge:	**Am I willing to** trust God for my well being.
Lesson:	God wants us to be thankful even in the difficult things.
Challenge:	**Am I willing to** be thankful even in the difficult things I face today?
Lesson:	I am fearfully and wonderfully made.
Challenge:	**Do I believe that** I am fearfully and wonderfully made?
Challenge:	**Am I willing to** view myself as fearfully and wonderfully made?

Notice that sometimes more than one *Challenge* may occur to you as you think about a *Lesson*. That is ok, in fact it is great. That means you are engaging your creativity and are seeing more parts of your life the *Lesson* can help.

Assignment 5

Motivation

1. Do I want to know God?

2. How do I want my life to be?

3. Do I want to do His will for my life?

4. Do I want to please God?

5. Do I want to know His heart and what He cares about?

6. Would I prefer my independence over His will and way?

7. It might change my priorities. What do I really want?

Continue to ponder these seven questions and the three verses: *Ephesians 3:16-19, Matthew 12:30-31,* and *Luke 18:13.* Explore the questions you hesitate on and see if you can untangle what is holding you back.

Skill

Flicker Philippians 1:9-11. Write out the *Facts, Lessons, Challenges,* and *Responses* in the *FLCR* panels provided on the next couple of pages.

Also, read the Appendix titled *Finding the Time.* This gives you some fresh thoughts about how to find time in your schedule for having a regular Time with God.

If you get stuck on *Philippians 1:9-11* you can check the Appendix titled *Answers* for some ideas.

Philippians 1:9 And this I pray, that your love may abound still more and more in real knowledge and all discernment,

Philippians 1:10 so that you may approve the things that are excellent, in order to be sincere and blameless until the day of Christ;

Philippians 1:11 having been filled with the fruit of righteousness which [comes] through Jesus Christ, to the glory and praise of God. (NASB)

Lessons

Challenges

Responses

"Don't put
your parent's face
on God."

The Authors

Chapter 6
Stretching Your Comfort Zone

Surfing was very popular when I [N] was growing up in Southern California so I gave it a try. Wow, I can still see the first time a wave lifted me, I stood on the board, navigated to the shoulder of the wave and had my first long ride. It was exhilarating, it was refreshing, and it was fun.

But surfing takes place in a very small area of the wave. Surfing in a crowded area is much like driving on the freeway during rush hour. Everyone is tightly packed together, taking risks, and operating on a system of unwritten rules that go far beyond the motor vehicle code. Invariably at crowded surfing spots tempers would flare and fights would break out.

I loved surfing but as a young kid and an *Introvert*, I didn't want anything to do with the fights. So, I switched surfing styles from stand-up surfing to spooning (a style like boogie boarding). This provided a natural separation between me and the fighting element so I could surf within my comfort zone. The only problem was that spooning was not as fun as stand-up surfing.

As an adult, I spent 15 years out of state. When I returned to Southern California I was eager to get back into surfing. As I reoriented myself, I had to decide if I was going to continue spooning or go back to stand-up surfing. I was not a kid any more and the reasons I had avoided stand-up surfing seemed silly, so I got a surfboard and went for it.

Eventually the thing I dreaded happened—my board and a hot head's board touched and I found myself in an unavoidable fight in the water. Fortunately, I got the upper hand and was able to keep him at bay. But I hated the whole intimidation atmosphere where people threaten to kill each other over a bumped board.

As I drove home from the beach that day I faced a decision. How badly did I want to surf? Was I willing to go beyond my comfort zone and take on these kinds of people or not? It took a long time for me to sort this out and I came close to giving up surfing and taking up another kind of exercise.

But in the end I decided, as an adult, I could make choices that improved my situation, and I could go after what I really wanted. It just might be uncomfortable for a while.

So, I decided to improve my situation. I surfed at less crowded spots and honed my surfing skills. Then I went to more crowded spots and would sit in the midst of the lineup watching others position for the waves and take or yield right-of-way. As I watched, I discovered a whole network of unspoken rules that went way beyond the basic right-of-way rules in surfing. Eventually, I got to the place where I was comfortable surfing in crowded areas and could successfully negotiate the hotheads.

It is never easy to step out of your comfort zone. But, as an adult, you are able to make decisions that improve your situation and help you skillfully negotiate the discomfort until you reach the goal.

Review Motivation Assignment 5

1. Do I want to know God?

2. How do I want my life to be?

3. Do I want to do His will for my life?

4. Do I want to please God?

5. Do I want to know His heart and what He cares about?

6. Would I prefer my independence over His will and way?

7. It might change my priorities. What do I really want?

It is surprising how many people hesitate on question 4, "Do I want to please God?" Sometimes our *Family of Origin Issues (FOOI)* can play a big part in that.

FOOI can make us worry that we can't please God, that it might even be impossible to please God. If we had a critical parent we might worry that God is as critical as our parent was—never satisfied—always seeing the negative.

If we had a critical parent and they were also controlling, we might worry that God will also micromanage us and be too interfering. No one wants to sign up for pleasing someone who is intrusive and almost impossible to please.

So, is God impossible to please? If you just look around at all God's sinful children you should be able to see that He does not micromanage us! He wants loving and obedient children who volunteer to love and obey Him.

Biblical Comfort Zone Examples

All the great people of the Bible faced fears. They all had to move out of their comfort zone: Abraham, Joseph, Jacob, Samuel, Moses, Daniel, David, Paul, and Peter. But there are two Bible characters that did not move out of their comfort zone. And though their lives started out promising, they ended sadly.

The first of these is Solomon. He was the second son of David and Bathsheba. God does not look at pedigree and did not exclude Solomon from His blessing because of his parent's sin. Solomon asked for wisdom and God gave it to him, but he didn't always use it.

You know how sometimes you know the right thing to do, but you choose to do otherwise? Solomon focused his life on the pursuit of pleasure. He took in seven hundred wives and three hundred concubines and they brought their foreign gods with them.

This became a problem for Solomon. His pursuit of pleasure got him off course. Solomon spent his life chasing after the *Deceitful Desires* of sex, money, and things. Then, at the end of his life he threw up his hands and said of his efforts, *"all is vanity and striving after wind." (Ecclesiastes 1:14 NASB)* He misspent his life trying to hold onto comfort and pleasure instead of being willing to leave his comfort zone.

---

1. Solomon misspent his life trying to hold on to

_____ and

_____

The other Bible character that did not step out of his comfort zone was Saul. Saul was the most handsome man in Israel and God picked him to be their king. Saul was reluctant at first, but God transformed him for the task.

Then, instead of staying humble and obedient to accomplish what God had in mind, he became headstrong and disobedient. When he heard God planned to give his throne to David, he did not humble himself to accept God's consequences, but became obsessed and paranoid trying to protect his power. He spent his time and effort running around the country trying to kill David instead of asking God to protect his throne. He was not willing to leave his comfort zone and trust God with his life.

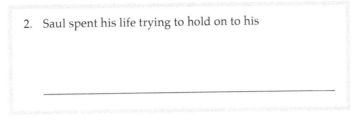

2. Saul spent his life trying to hold on to his

_____

Our job is to be a good steward of the life God gives us and be willing to step out of our comfort zone when called upon.

Introverts and Extroverts

Responding to God

Our *FOOI* can make it harder for us to obey God's word and step out of our comfort zone. For example, in *1 John 1:9* God challenges us that if we step out of our comfort zone (confess our sins), we will receive forgiveness. This verse is pretty straightforward but our background may slant how we respond to it.

> *1 John 1:9* **If we confess** *our sins, He is faithful and just and* **will forgive** *us our sins and purify us from all unrighteousness. (NIV1984)*

If you were never held accountable growing up, you will tend to blame others for your mistakes. This is called *Projection*. You *Project* blame onto others. You say, "My problems are someone else's fault."

If this is your tendency, when you read this verse you probably have trouble thinking of anything to confess because everything is someone else's fault. You push responsibility off yourself and onto others so you don't think the verse applies to you much.

3. *Extroverts* tend to

_____

On the other hand, when you were growing up, if you believed most things were your fault, you learn to *Introject*, or take on too much responsibility. You blame yourself inappropriately. This person says, "If the people around me are angry or sad, it is probably my fault."

People that approach life from this point of view worry they are really forgiven. When they come to *1 John 1:9* they have trouble believing that they have confessed well enough. Saying you are sorry to a critical parent doesn't usually help much.

4. *Introverts* tend to

_____

But *1 John 1:9* is very simple and straightforward. We confess—He is faithful and just to forgive. We complicate it with *FOOI*. It does not say He will forgive if we confess with just the right tone and expression on our face. We just have to confess, He is the faithful One and will forgive.

A balanced person takes responsibility for their sin, takes God at His word, and confesses. That's it.

5. A balanced person responds to the verse by taking

_____ for their sin, taking God at His

_____ and

_____

Know Your Tendency

I [D] have noticed in my private practice that *Introverts* tend to *Introject*. They tend to accept too much responsibility for a problem. *Extroverts* tend to *Project*. They don't accept enough responsibility. That's why *Extroverts* feel good most of the time—nothing is ever their fault.

Now there are balanced *Introverts* and balanced *Extroverts* who accept responsibility for their part and no more. It is helpful to notice your tendency so you can correct for it.

Noel is an *Introvert* and tends to *Introject*. I'm [D] more of an *Extrovert* and tend to *Project*. When we were first married I inadvertently got away with murder. I *Projected* and assigned the blame for things and he *Introjected* and accepted it! Then after a few years he wised up and figured it couldn't always be all his fault. Now it is better for both of us. It is better for me to be accountable for my part so I can grow, and it is better for him not to be shouldering all the blame.

Making Someone Mad?

Let me [D] say a word to those of you who *Introject* and accept too much responsibility. In our culture it is common to hear the phrase, "You make me so mad." That is an over-statement. You don't have the power to make anyone mad without their permission.

When our kids were in school, one of their teachers always got under my skin. Every time I was around him, I found myself getting angry. Then one day I had too much going on to be reacting to him, so I decided to be apathetic about his behavior that day. That was the day I first realized that he didn't have the power to make me angry. His behavior was irritating, but I did not have to be irritated. It wasn't worth the effort.

Have you ever tried to cheer up someone who doesn't want to be cheered up? Has anyone tried to cheer you up when you weren't done being angry or sad? You are not going to be cheered up until you decide you are ready. You are the only person with control over your emotions.

We don't have power to control another person's emotions. Some people have allowed themselves to become very reactive to everyone around them, but they are choosing to be reactive. They could learn to be more apathetic to some of the stimulus around them.

You are *not* responsible for someone else's anger. You *are* responsible for your own behavior.

6. You do not have the power to make someone

_____

Humility is Answer for Both

Humility is the answer for both the *Introvert* and the *Extrovert*. If you *Introject* and accept too much blame, you need to know your limits. Humble yourself and realize you are not as powerful as you think. You can not control the people around you.

If you *Project* and don't accept enough blame, you need to humble yourself and take responsibility for your sins. You are not perfect.

7. The answer for both the *Introvert* and the *Extravert* is

_____

Get to Know God

The best way to keep your *FOOI* from distorting your experience with God is to get to know God.

For example, if you find you are having trouble trusting God, see if you are reacting to Him like you reacted to one of your parents. If so, contrast what that parent is like against what God is like. The better you know God, the better you will neutralize your *FOOI*. He is certainly different than your parents. Keep adding to your list of what God is like (see page 115).

In *Psalm 34:18-19* God reminds us how strong and compassionate He is. He delivers us from all our troubles.

> *Psalm 34:18-19 The Lord is* **close** *to the brokenhearted and* **saves** *those who are crushed in spirit. A righteous man may have many troubles, but the Lord* **delivers** *him from them* **all***; (NIV1984)*

8. God is strong and

_____

Dr. Tony Evans said when he was a boy, his parents got him a punching bag that sat on the floor and would rock back and forth as he punched on it. One day he punched it so hard it ricocheted around the room, bouncing off the walls, boom, boom, boom, until it finally righted itself on the floor and began to sway back and forth, bing, bing, bing—bink!

He said that is what life can seem like at times. We are ricocheting off the walls of life, bouncing around, but God will right us. We will go boom, boom, boom, bing, bing, bing—bink! He delivers us from all our troubles. When you need to move beyond your comfort zone it is good to know that God is right there promising to deliver you.

Getting to know God will smooth out your *FOOI* and it will provide true comfort that is absent from *Deceitful Desires*. According to *2 Corinthians 1:3-4*, God is the Father of compassion and the God of all comfort.

> *2 Corinthians 1:3-4 Praise be to the God and Father of our Lord Jesus Christ, the **Father of compassion** and the **God of all comfort**, who comforts us in all our troubles, so that we can comfort those in any trouble with the comfort we ourselves have received from God. (NIV1984)*

9. God is the Father of compassion and the God of all

_____

Are you looking to God for comfort? He stands ready to give it. Or are you looking to something else for comfort: a new gadget or car, the mall, food, TV, work, or leisure?

It took all of us awhile to select what we turn to for comfort. We didn't just instantly know the foods that would provide the most comfort, or the best videos or TV shows to watch to cheer us up. We figured that out by experimenting. We need to do the same thing when turning to God for comfort. It might take you awhile to figure out how to read the Bible and ask God specifically for comfort, but it is worth the effort.

As you practice asking God for comfort, take note of your attitude. Do you have a chip on your shoulder and a resistance to being "cheered up?" If you aren't ready to be cheered up, you won't allow God to comfort you. Get you attitude ready, then look to God for comfort.

10. Looking to God for comfort will take

_____

Review Skill Assignment 5

One of the *Skill* assignments was to read the Appendix titled *Finding the Time*. Our lives are already so packed, it can be a real challenge to figure out where to put your Time with God.

Be sure to notice that I [N] am taking a different tact than is usually taken to this problem. Rather than suggesting that you cram your Time with God into a place that is already full and make it work, I am suggesting that you wipe your slate clean and figure out where a Time with God would work the best for you ideally. Then see if you can wrap the rest of your life around it. Most people don't even try this. They assume it couldn't possibly work in an ideal time slot. I am encouraging you to be brave and go for ideal first.

The other assignment was to *Flicker Philippians 1:9*.

> *Philippians 1:9 And this I pray, that your love may abound still more and more in real knowledge and all discernment,*
>
> *Philippians 1:10 so that you may approve the things that are excellent, in order to be sincere and blameless until the day of Christ;*
>
> *Philippians 1:11 having been filled with the fruit of righteousness which [comes] through Jesus Christ, to the glory and praise of God. (NASB)*

Your *Facts* for this passage probably identified things like "This is a prayer," "He is talking about their love," and "He wants it to increase." That is excellent! You are right on track.

There are several *Lessons* in this passage (for more examples see the Appendix titled *Answers)*. But what did you make out of the phrase in the last part of *verse 9 "in real knowledge and all discernment"*? It seems unusual to me that he wants their love to increase in knowledge and discernment.

Usually you associate love with an emotion or an action of service. In the usual case increasing love means developing stronger emotions or undertaking larger-scale actions of service. But how does a person's love increase in knowledge and discernment? These are ways of thinking and judging not feeling and serving. Maybe you could *Learn* that "he wants their emotions and acts of service to increase in the content and discernment of what they do."

Turning that *Lesson* into a *Challenge,* "Am I willing to be more discerning in the way I give?"—like giving a gift certificate for McDonnalds to someone asking for food or offering to buy something to eat for them rather than just giving cash? As you think about this, I'll bet you come up with other *Challenges.*

If we were together in a group I would love to hear what you were able to *Learn* from this passage. There is nothing like *Flickering* a passage in a group.

Flicker Practice

Flicker the short verses on the following pages. Write your answers in the provided *FLCR* panels.

If you get stuck you can check the Appendix titled *Answers* for some ideas.

Romans 8:31-32

Facts

Romans 8:31 What then shall we say to these things? If God [is] for us, who [is] against us?

Romans 8:32 He who did not spare His own Son, but delivered Him over for us all, how will He not also with Him freely give us all things? (NASB)

Lessons

Challenges

Responses

1 Peter 1:24   For, "ALL FLESH IS LIKE GRASS, AND ALL ITS GLORY LIKE THE FLOWER OF GRASS. THE GRASS WITHERS, AND THE FLOWER FALLS OFF,

1 Peter 1:25   BUT THE WORD OF THE LORD EN-DURES FOREVER." And this is the word which was preached to you. (NASB)

Lessons

Challenges

Responses

About Flicker Practice

We have been *Flickering* shorter passages of one and two verses. You may be curious if you can *Flicker* longer passages. The answer is a resounding yes! Shorter passages are easier for most people to work with when they are starting out.

When you *Flicker* any length passage you mentally divide the passage into *Sections* and focus on each section to get the *Facts,* etc. When you *Flicker* longer passages, what changes is the length of the *Sections.*

When *Flickering* a passage of one or two verses, the *Sections* usually consist of a single word or maybe a short phrase. When *Flickering* a passage of three to ten verses you should mentally break it into larger *Sections* consisting of a few verses each. As the passage gets longer, your *Flicker* statements start summarizing more material. You start focusing on the larger movements in the story.

When *Flickering* a passage that is a whole chapter, the *Sections* should basically be paragraphs, i.e. three to six verses each. It is like flying in an airliner. Before take off you are focusing on people and luggage and terminal gates. Just after you take off your focus shifts to cars and buildings, then when you get higher you focus on the large colored parcels of land. You still take in about the same amount, but the information is more summary in nature.

It is important to realize that a *Flicker* session should always take about the same amount of time regardless how large the passage is.

Can you *Flicker* larger passages, yes. If your passage is a whole book, the *Sections* are groups of chapters. If your passage is the whole Bible (yes, it's possible), the *Sections* are groups of books.

Assignment 6

Motivation

1. Do I want to know God?

2. How do I want my life to be?

3. Do I want to do His will for my life?

4. Do I want to please God?

5. Do I want to know His heart and what He cares about?

6. Would I prefer my independence over His will and way?

7. It might change my priorities. What do I really want?

Continue to ponder these seven questions and the three verses: *Ephesians 3:16-19, Matthew 12:30-31,* and *Luke 18:13.* Explore the questions you hesitate on and see if you can untangle what is holding you back.

Skill

Flicker Mark 10:13-16. Write out the *Facts, Lessons, Challenges,* and *Responses* in the *FLCR* panels provided on the next couple of pages.

Also, read the Appendix titled *Answering Your Questions.* Although it is not a good idea to focus on the things you do not know, sometimes a question can become a stumbling block. For those times, this Appendix gives you steps and attitudes to take to find your answer.

If you get stuck on *Mark 10:13-16* you can check the Appendix titled *Answers* for some ideas.

Mark 10:13 And they were bringing children to Him so that He might touch them; but the disciples rebuked them.

Mark 10:14 But when Jesus saw this, He was indignant and said to them, "Permit the children to come to Me; do not hinder them; for the kingdom of God belongs to such as these.

Mark 10:15 "Truly I say to you, whoever does not receive the kingdom of God like a child will not enter it [at] [all.]"

Mark 10:16 And He took them in His arms and [began] blessing them, laying His hands on them. (NASB)

Lessons

Challenges

Responses

"Don't focus
on the mountain."

Bill Hybels

www.WaveStudyBible.com Chapter 7

Chapter 7
Aligning Your Prayers

I saw fear in her eyes. It was the week after High School graduation and I [N] was expecting to see relief and celebration. But our oldest daughter was showing signs of apprehension about her upcoming entrance into college.

Even though she had been a good student in High School, the transition to college was full of uncertainty. Would she know what classes to take? Would she be successful? So many things would be on her shoulders.

As I thought about her situation, I came up with an activity that would channel some of that energy into a task that might help her confidence. I asked her to get her college catalog and we found the place that discussed her major. Then I said, "Everything you need to know about graduating from college is described in these pages. I want you to read them and be able to explain the requirements for graduation. I will expect you to know things like the meaning of 'General Education' units. In one week I will quiz you."

I expected to get resistance from her, but to my surprise, she smiled and acted grateful to have a direction. When she was ready, we opened the college catalog again and I asked her to explain how to graduate. When she used technical terms, like "GE" units, I asked her to explain what they meant. If she did not know, we looked into the catalog together and found the answer. I used the same strategy with each of our four kids after they graduated from High School.

Since they were all aligned to what the college offered them and expected from them, they all graduated from college—three of them graduating in four years.

There is no substitute for aligning yourself with the plan.

Review Motivation Assignment 5

1. Do I want to know God?

2. How do I want my life to be?

3. Do I want to do His will for my life?

4. Do I want to please God?

5. Do I want to know His heart and what He cares about?

6. Would I prefer my independence over His will and way?

7. It might change my priorities. What do I really want?

If you hesitate on question 5 above, *Family of Origin Issues* *(FOOI)* may be slanting you in that direction.

For example, If you had a care-taking role in your family growing up, you may worry that if you decide you want to know God's heart, and what He cares about, that you will feel too much pain. It is likely you don't want to take on any more responsibility because trying to help people feel better in your *Family Of Origin* was a full time job. Plus, if you are currently helping your husband or children feel better you can worry you don't have the emotional room to add what God cares about.

What you may be missing is God is not like your parents or siblings or husband or children. His heart is love and light. He is not dark, moody or depressed. Everything good in the world originated from Him. He looks at a problem and offers love, redemption and healing. He wants us to rejoice in everything *(1 Thessalonians 5:18)* because He has this. This is His heart. He wants us to always know we are well no matter the problems. He is working out His will.

Seeing His heart and what He cares about is instructive and liberating.

Prayer in Three Steps

God wants to hear from us and He wants to grant our requests. He has included a number of passages in the Bible to help us know how to pray in a way He can answer.

There are basically three steps in prayer:

1. Align with God

2. Ask for what you want

3. Prepare to receive it

1. There are three steps in prayer:

_____

_____

_____

When you first begin, that is all you need to know to pray to our heavenly Father. As you want to get more effective praying, begin to explore each of these steps in more detail. As some of the concepts like *Abiding* or *Forgiving* start making sense to you, begin to incorporate them in your prayers.

Expand gradually. Do not let yourself be overwhelmed with the details, but progress fast enough to keep yourself challenged. Prayer is simple enough that anyone can do it and powerful enough to challenge the most proficient to new heights.

---

2. Prayer is simple enough that

_____

There is no lack of challenge when tapping the potential of prayer. Jesus said if we prayed with faith the size of a mustard seed, we could move a mountain from here to there and that nothing would be impossible for us. *(Matthew 17:20)*

We all have needs. As God goes around causing all things to work together for good *(Romans 8:28)* He loves to incorporate answers to the prayers we make.

The better we learn to pray, the more God is able to answer our prayers.

Step 1: Align with God

This is the step where we make a conscious effort to connect with God and see things from His point of view. This will help us align our wants to God's wants and recognize God's answers when they come.

> 3. This is the step where we
>
> _____

This alignment step is described in many ways in the Bible. The following sections will cover the most important ones. You shouldn't feel the need to tackle all of these at once. Just look them over and explore one or two that will challenge your current prayer life.

Remember, the goal of *Step 1* is to connect with God and start to see things from His perspective.

In Jesus' Name

In *John 16:23* the Bible says that if we ask anything in the name of Jesus, we will receive it.

> *John 16:23* *"Truly, truly, I say to you, if you ask the Father for anything **in My name**, He will give it to you. (NASB)*

This means that as we talk to a God, if we are praying in Jesus' name, we recognize that there is only one reason a sinful human being can speak directly with a sinless holy God—because Jesus paid for our sins and clothes us with righteousness.

4. We will receive anything we ask for when we ask

_____

5. Praying *In Jesus Name* means to approach God recognizing that

_____

The only reason we have access to God is because of what Jesus did. So we approach God with the name of Jesus on our lips understanding that He made this access possible.

God wants us to pray in Jesus' name.

According to God's Will

Another description of how to align with God for effective prayer is to ask for what God wants to give us. Notice 1 John 5:14-15.

> 1 John 5:14-15 *This is the confidence which we have before Him, that, if we ask anything **according to His will**, He hears us. And if we know that He hears us [in] whatever we ask, we know that we have the requests which we have asked from Him. (NASB)*

There are many things that God has promised and wants to give us. We just have to get on the same page. He really loves it when we are so aligned with Him that what we want is what He wants to give us.

6. Praying *According to God's Will* is to ask for what God already wants

_____

Bible prayers are the easiest way to be sure we are asking for things according to His will. There are three Bible prayers I [D] like to pray back to God during my Time with Him. It has been amazing to see how well this simple activity has aligned my thinking with His values.

7. The easiest way to pray *According to God's Will* is to pray

_____

The first prayer is from *Ephesians 1:17-21* which I have paraphrased the way I pray it.

> "Please give me a spirit of wisdom and revelation in the knowledge of You. May the eyes of my heart be enlightened so I will know what is the hope of Your calling, the riches of the glory of Your inheritance to the saints, and what is the surpassing greatness of Your power toward us who believe. You used this power when You raised Christ from the dead and seated Him at Your right hand in heaven, far above all rule and authority, power and dominion" (paraphrased from *Ephesians 1:17-21* NIV)

The second prayer is from *Ephesians 3:14-20.*

> "I bow my knees before You Father, from whom every family in heaven and on earth derives its name. Please grant me, according to the riches of Your glory, to be strengthened with power through Your Spirit in the inner man, so that Christ may dwell in my heart through faith; and that I will be rooted and grounded in love, able to comprehend with all the saints what is the breadth and length and height and depth and to know the love of Christ which surpasses knowledge, filled up to all the fullness of God. Now to You who are able to do far more abundantly beyond all that I ask or think, according to the power that works within me, to Him be the glory in the church and in Christ Jesus to all generations forever and ever." (paraphrase of *Ephesians 3:14-20* NIV)

The third prayer comes from *Colossians 1:9-12.*

> "Please fill me with the knowledge of Your will in all spiritual wisdom and understanding, so that I will walk in a manner worthy of You Lord, to please You in all respects, bearing fruit in every good work and increasing in the knowledge of You. Please strengthen me with all power, according to Your glorious might, for the attaining of all steadfastness and patience; joyously giving thanks to You Father, who qualified

me to share in the inheritance of the saints in Light." (paraphrase of *Colossians 1:9-12* NIV)

As you pray these back to God, it aligns your thinking with what God considers important and helpful. If we pray anything according to His will, we know that we have our requests in His time.

Forgive and Be Forgiven

To pray effectively, we need to be free from the distraction of sin.

8. He wants to free us from the burden of harboring

_____

He wants to lift us from the burden of our own sins. He will not hear us if we are holding on to our sin *(Psalm 66:18)* and He stands ready to hear our confession of sins in prayer *(1 John 1:9)* and forgive them.

> *Psalm 66:18 If I **regard wickedness** in my heart, The Lord will not hear; (NASB)*

> *1 John 1:9 **If we confess** our sins, **He is faithful** and righteous **to forgive** us our sins and to cleanse us from all unrighteousness. (NASB)*

He also wants to free us of the burden of harboring resentment toward others. When Jesus taught his disciples how to pray in *Matthew 6:12* He included this as an important ingredient in effective prayer.

> *Matthew 6:12 'And forgive us our debts, **as we also have forgiven our debtors.** (NASB)*

Some transgressions are easier to forgive than others. For the hard ones, God wants you to consciously decide that the other person is not responsible to you. Turn them over to God saying, "Lord you deal with them, they are responsible to you." Otherwise you are stuck waiting for them to make amends.

> 9. When you forgive someone, you are resigning from being their

Don't worry about your negative feelings coming back. When they do, just turn them back over to God again. Eventually the negative feelings will die down.

Your most effective prayers will confess any known sins and forgive any people who have wronged you. When you "forgive" someone, you are not saying their offense did not matter. You are resigning from being judge and jury and allowing God to handle it. You use your energy to trust God to do the right thing, even if things aren't going your way now.

Abide in Jesus

The Bible describes prayer as coming close to God, adapting to what He values, and wanting the same thing. You let God rub off on you and ask Him for what you want.

In *John 15:4,7* God urges us to find that place and camp out there.

> *John 15:4,7 "Abide in Me, and I in you. As the branch cannot bear fruit of itself unless it abides in the vine, so neither [can] you unless you abide in Me.* **"If you abide in Me, and My words abide in you, ask whatever you wish, and it will be done for you.** *(NASB)*

The word that is translated *abide* means to remain, to hang out, to spend time at a place you don't want to leave.

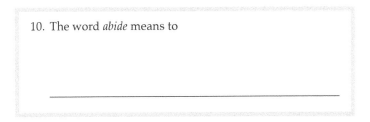

10. The word *abide* means to

_____

This is what happens to me [N] every time I come across a hobby store. I go into the store. I relax and marvel at the airplanes hanging from the ceiling. I study the new radio control airplanes on display to see if they meet my need. But most importantly, I *abide* there—indefinitely. I never want to leave. Even after I go, the experience still lingers with me.

God says to *abide* in Jesus as the branch *abides* in the vine. A branch does more than hang out with the vine. A branch also is connected to the vine. In prayer, we are to connect with God as our source of strength and as the one to whom we belong. Just like the branch soaks in nutrients from the vine, we are to soak in how much He loves us. We are to open up to Him and linger there. That is the perspective of effective prayer.

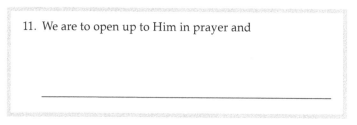

11. We are to open up to Him in prayer and

_____

Delight in the Lord

One of the most effective ways to align with God in prayer is to identify the qualities of God that you love. In *Psalm 37:4* David says this is an attitude God can respond to.

> *Psalms 37:4* **Delight yourself in the LORD**; *And He will give you the desires of your heart. (NASB)*

God is your treasure. He is the one thing you can count on. God is asking you to treasure your relationship with Him as the most valuable thing in your life.

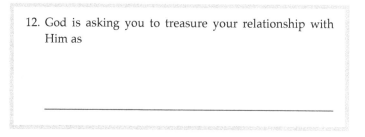

12. God is asking you to treasure your relationship with Him as

_____

You delight in Him because you can always count on Him: He is holy and will always do the right thing for you. He is love so He will do it with love.

To delight in God means you are fully satisfied and pleased with Him. He is your treasure. It means you see Him as your security and you simply trust Him. You want His will over your own will. You have a deep sense of satisfaction knowing He will keep you.

13. To *Delight in God* means you are fully satisfied and

_____ with Him.

If you delight in Him, you see Him as all good, all powerful, and in charge of you and He will give you the desires of your heart.

Worship the Lord

As we pray and think about what the Lord is like our natural response is to worship Him. Jesus talks about our worship of God in *Luke 4:8.*

> *Luke 4:8 Jesus answered him, "It is written, 'YOU SHALL* **WORSHIP THE LORD YOUR GOD** *AND SERVE HIM ONLY.'" (NASB)*

Worship is our response when we get a glimpse of who He is and what He has done for us. If we just get an inkling of the magnitude of the inheritance God has prepared for us in heaven, we become filled with gratitude and worship Him in prayer.

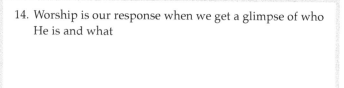

14. Worship is our response when we get a glimpse of who He is and what

God has sealed us in the Holy Spirit, placed us safely in Christ Jesus, He guides our footsteps, and has already prepared good works for us to walk in. He just wants us to co-operate, to trust Him, and to want His will and wait for it.

He has it all planned out. He doesn't want us to work against Him. We are to get to know Him and understand His great sacrifice for us. If we get a hold of that we will be grateful and cooperative.

As you explore what God is like in prayer, you will know you are aligning with Him if you find yourself responding in worship to Him.

Meditate on Who God Is

God values meditation. This is not the kind of meditation where you focus your mind on emptiness or oneness as is popular in some circles. This kind of meditation focuses your mind on what the Lord is like. Listen to David's description of meditation in *Psalm 1:2*.

> *Psalm 1:2 But his delight is in the law of the LORD, And* **in His law he meditates day and night.** *(NASB)*

God reveals what He is like in every part of scripture. As you have been studying Abraham, you have been making a list of what God is like. Meditate on those qualities of God surfaced from studying His word.

At the time David wrote *Psalm 1*, most of the Bible had not been written. The clearest unit of scriptures available to him was known as *the law*, which consisted of the first five books of the Bible: *Genesis, Exodus, Leviticus, Numbers,* and *Deuteronomy*. Now we have the entire Bible and there is value meditating on all of it.

Meditation is most effective for those who respond well to visualization.

15. Meditation is most effective for those who respond well to

_____

This is an opportunity to visualize what God is like by picturing Him with the qualities on your list. Someone who has the qualities listed here as well as the qualities you have added to the list from your study.

- God is slow to anger
  (Exodus 34:6)

- God's mercies are new every morning
  (Lamentations 3:23)

- God is rich in kindness
  (Exodus 34:6)

- God is Holy
  (1 Samuel 2:2, Isaiah 6:3)

- God always does what is right
  (Genesis 18:25)

- God is perfect
  (Deuteronomy 32:4)

- God is not needy
  (Acts 17:25)

- God is love
  (1 John 4:8)

- God never sins when He is angry
  (Deuteronomy 32:4)

- God made a way for me to be forgiven
  (John 3:16)

- God has my best interest in mind
  (Luke 11:13)

It can be helpful to focus on those qualities that are different from your parents. Meditating and visualizing these qualities helps to update your relationship with God.

Remember, if you are an adult, your world is not controlled by your earthly *Family Of Origin*. Rather, you live in a world controlled by your heavenly Father. His love, kindness, and strength define the context in which you live. In a very real sense, "This is my Father's world."

Besides visualizing God, you can continue the picture by visualizing yourself as God sees you and visualize the way

Jesus connects us to God. To visualize yourself as God sees you, there would be an image of someone that was worth the ultimate sacrifice to redeem them from destruction.

To complete the picture, introduce the sin concept. View God as holy and yourself as separated from Him by the presence of sin. Then Jesus enters the picture, pays for our sin, and wraps you in His righteousness. This help to illustrate that our only path to God is through Jesus which is what it means to pray in Jesus name.

Keep in mind that some people really benefit from visualizing concepts like this. If you *do* benefit from visualization, this can help establish your context as you come to God.

Each of these descriptions in *Step 1* have presented a dimension of how to connect with God during your prayer time. In some prayer sessions you will be more successful with *Step 1* than in others. Seek to increase your effectiveness with this step. It sets the context for your prayer session.

Step 2: Ask for What You Want

After you align with God, you are ready to bring your requests to God. A prayer session does not always need to include requests for what you need. From time to time, you may be in a very good place where you don't feel the need to ask for anything. But you are probably aware of needs that the people around you have. Learn how to effectively ask God to meet needs.

Just like in *Step 1*, this step includes several descriptions of how to ask for what you want. Each of these descriptions give you another perspective from which to view effective petitioning. Don't try to incorporate all of these into your prayer life at once. Rather choose something that challenges you and work with that for a while. Then try another one. Always aim to keep yourself challenged without being overwhelmed.

Pray the Promises

The first description of effective petitioning urges us to focus on God's *Promises*. Don't pray the problems—pray the *Promises*.

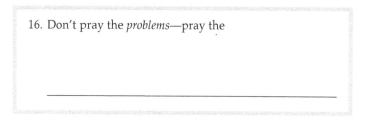

16. Don't pray the *problems*—pray the

If you focus on the problem and just repeat it back to God, you are rehearsing the problem in your head. No wonder you finish praying and don't feel too much better. Instead, find a *Promise* in God's Word that applies to your problem and pray the *Promise*.

For example, let's say it is getting close to the end of the month, you are running out of money, and the bills are still stacked on your desk. A common way to pray is to wring your hands and say, "Oh Lord, You see all these bills and I am out of money. I don't know what to do." As you continue to pray, you just keep repeating that in different ways to the Lord. At the end of your prayer time, you have completely rehearsed the magnitude of the problem over and over.

A better way to pray is to align with the *Promises* God has made concerning your problem. The Appendix titled *Promises* on page 209 lists a number of these Bible *Promises* by category. Under the category of *Need for Success or Prosperity* the following *Promises* are listed.

> *Philippians 4:19 And my **God will supply all your needs** according to His riches in glory in Christ Jesus. (NASB)*
>
> *Matthew 6:30-33 "But if God so clothes the grass of the field, which is [alive] today and tomorrow is thrown into the furnace, [will He] not much more [clothe] you? You of little faith! Do not worry then, saying, 'What will we eat?' or 'What will we drink?' or 'What will we wear for clothing?' For the Gentiles eagerly seek all these things; for your heavenly Father knows that you need all these things. **But seek first His kingdom and His righteousness, and all these things will be added to you.**" (NASB)*

The best way to align with these *Promises* is to use your own words to pray the *Promise* back to God saying something like this.

> Lord, thank You for promising to supply all my needs according to Your riches in Christ Jesus. My hope is in You. Thank You that You always keep Your promises. (paraphrase of Philippians 4:19 NASB)
>
> Lord, forgive me for worrying about these bills. Thank You that You know what I need. Help me to seek You, Your kingdom, and Your righteousness first. Thank

You for taking care of everything else. (paraphrase of Matthew 6:30-33 NASB)

Praying back to God a *Promise* He has made, aligns us with what He has *Promised* to do. As a result, we move from rehearsing the problem to trusting a *Promise* God has made.

17. Praying a Bible *promise* aligns us with what He has

_____

With Thanksgiving

God wants us to be thankful as we ask for what we want (*Philippians 4:6*).

> *Philippians 4:6 Be anxious for nothing, but in everything by prayer and supplication **with thanksgiving** let your requests be made known to God. (NASB)*

If your kids come to you already grateful for what you have given them, they ask for the next thing in a way that makes it easy to grant their request.

When we come to God grateful and appreciative, it puts us in the perspective where we know God will do what is right for us because He has already been good to us. When our glass is half full, we feel optimistic about our next request.

God is really generous and doesn't mind us asking. He likes to give and He likes us to know He can give. He just wants us to come believing that He has our best interest in mind. Praying with thanksgiving strengthens our relationship with God.

18. God likes to give and He likes us to know that

_____

With Boldness

In *Hebrews 4:16* God encourages us to come to Him boldly in prayer.

> *Hebrews 4:16 Let us therefore come **boldly** unto the throne of grace, that we may obtain mercy, and find grace to help in time of need. (KJV)*

For some personalities, it is second nature to ask for things boldly but for others it is a very new idea.

Asking God for things boldly does not mean praying with disrespect. It means to ask with the assurance that God accepts you and that He does not get irritated. He wants you to say what is on your mind clearly, freely, and without hesitation. This is what *He* wants.

---

19. Praying with *Boldness* means to ask clearly, freely, and without

_____

If you have not tried praying with boldness, you will be surprised how clear your petition becomes. Give it a try.

With Persistence

God encourages us to ask Him repeatedly for things by telling these unusual stories about a widow pestering the unjust judge *(Luke 18:1-7)* and a neighbor who comes in the middle of the night for bread *(Luke 11:5-10)*. God wants us to keep coming to Him.

For some people, their *Family Of Origin Issues (FOOI)* can hinder their willingness to ask persistently.

For example, if you had a dominating parent who would never bend, it can be hard to repeatedly ask God for things. We might think, "What's the use, He has made up His mind." If God doesn't answer our prayer right away, we are tempted to fill in the reason from our past experience.

Why didn't we get what we wanted in the past? Was our parent uninvolved? Did they favor another sibling more? We assume God has not answered our prayer today for the same reason. But we are usually very far from the truth.

> 20. If God doesn't answer our prayer right away, we are tempted to fill in the reason from
>
> _____

Instead of contaminating the present with past experiences, we should look to understand what God is like, and interpret the unanswered prayer in light of the way God is.

Sometimes, when you don't want to keep asking God for the same thing it can be a defense. You just don't want to get whacked for being irritating.

Other times it can be pride and a desire to be independent. "Why should I have to keep asking? He knows what I want." It is a disconnect.

The harsh parent pushes you away by saying, "Don't ask me again. Leave me alone." God pulls you close by saying "stay with Me, keep asking, stay connected, depend on Me, I won't let you down." He is the opposite of a harsh parent. He wants to be close. He likes you to ask and stay connected.

> 21. God is the opposite of a harsh parent. He likes you to ask and
>
> _____

One strategy is to tell the Lord, "I am going to keep asking You for this unless You change my heart."

One of the many benefits of a heart fully committed to God is found in *2 Chronicles 16:9a*. You can ask God for strength to encourage you when an answer to a prayer is slow coming.

> *2 Chronicles 16:9a For the eyes of the Lord range throughout the earth to strengthen **those whose hearts are fully committed to him**. (NIV1984)*

For example, when we put our house up for sale, we expected it to sell on the first day because it had sold in one day when we bought it. But days and weeks passed without success. I [D] asked God for encouragement when it hadn't stirred any interest in the first month. He led me to the passage where Elizabeth found out she was pregnant with John the Baptist at about 90 years of age! I burst into tears and said, "What are you saying Lord? I'm going to be 90 when the house sells?" I asked Noel about it and he said the Lord was probably saying that the house was going to take "longer than normal" to sell. Well, that interpretation turned out to be right. But, God has a sense of humor. The house sold in 9 months. I wish I hadn't focused so much on Elizabeth's age so I could see the other possibility!

Pray God's promises. He keeps His Word. He will increase your patience and steadfastness as you wait, and your faith will skyrocket when you see Him keeping His promises to meet your needs. His solutions are always far better than our forced attempts.

With Patience

Waiting is very beneficial. This is how we develop patience and steadfastness—two of God's favorite qualities in us. When we know He will meet all our needs and it's a done deal, we know joy is on the way. In *Hebrews 12:2* Jesus showed us how.

> *Hebrews 12:2* ...*who **for the joy** set before Him endured the cross **despising the shame**, and has sat down at the right hand of the throne of God."*

Jesus knew joy was coming. So even though He despised the shame, He kept the joy set before Him and endured. When we are waiting, we would do well to know that joy is on the way. God wants us to have expectant hope. Are you aware of God's promises to you and the inheritance He has prepared? Is today the day when God's answer comes? It is just a matter of time before you see God's deliverance for you. Jesus was clear on the joy set before Him. Are you?

22. When we are waiting, we would do well to know that

_____

With Help from the Holy Spirit

It can be a great experience to feel yourself align with God in prayer. But it is important to realize that your feelings do not tell the whole story.

In *Romans 8:26* God says when you pray, the Holy Spirit interprets your prayers directly to God in a deep and effective way.

> *Romans 8:26 In the same way the Spirit also helps our weakness; for we do not know how to pray as we should, but* **the Spirit Himself intercedes for [us]** *with groanings too deep for words; (NASB)*

The wording used indicates that the Holy Spirit really cares and is going to great lengths (groaning). This is not a flippant prayer. but a deep heartfelt concern for us and for what we are concerned about.

So, remember when you pray, there is a lot going on under the hood. Your prayer's effectiveness does not depend on how accurately you pray. The Holy Spirit is translating your prayer and communicating with God with complete accuracy.

23. While you are praying, the Holy Spirit is translating your prayer with complete

_____

With Faith

When we ask God for things, He wants us to believe we will receive them *(Matthew 21:22)*.

> *Matthew 21:22 "And all things you ask in prayer, **believing**, you will receive." (NASB)*

Think of it from the opposite point of view. If your child came to you, not believing you really cared or had their best interest in mind, it would be a bad experience for you both. In the same way it is a bad experience for you to ask God for something when you don't really trust Him. It is also bad for God because He is dishonored.

This is not what God wants. He wants you to ask in faith knowing He loves you and He can do it. He wants a relationship of trust, gratitude, and faith.

How do you know that you are asking in faith? If you are asking in faith, it will makes sense to start preparing to receive your request.

24. If you are asking in faith, it will make sense to start preparing to

_____

Step 3: Prepare to Receive It

The third step in prayer is a reality check. This step identifies whether you were praying to God or just mouthing the words? If you were praying to God, it will feel appropriate in many cases to do something to prepare to receive God's answer.

25. If we expect an answer, many times there is something we can do to prepare a way to

_____

In the excellent Christian block buster movie, *Facing the Giants*, the story is told of two farmers who desperately needed rain. Both farmers prayed for rain but only one of them prepared his field to receive the rain.

Which farmer prayed for rain in faith? Well, the one that was willing to put his faith into action is the one who prayed in faith. Which one are you?

Faith is not passive. If we really expect an answer, many times there is something we can do as an act of faith to prepare the way for the answer.

By saying this, we are not suggesting that you neglect the responsible part that you play in the equation. If you have a ton of debt, it would not be responsible to pray for money then go out and spend further into debt as an act of faith. But, just like the farmer, there are often ways that are consistent with being responsible that allow you to put your faith into action.

God wants us to expect His provision and He wants us to do our part. Our part isn't that big but it is important. When we do our part, it gets our mind right and our attitude right. We start thinking more ideally. We start thinking more eternally minded.

Preparing to receive God's answer to our prayer gets us more focused on God's timing and provision, rather than just focusing on what we need.

Are you preparing for rain?

---

26. Preparing to receive God's answer to our prayer gets us more focused on

_____

Review Skill Assignment 6

One of the *Skill* assignments was to read the Appendix titled *Answering Your Questions*. That gives steps for what to do when you are forced into a box and need to answer one of your questions to go forward.

The psychology of learning tells us that if you ask a question and immediately get the answer to it, in 15 minutes you will have forgotten the question and the answer. The most important part of answering your own question is to find out what you think the best answer is first. Then when you seek outside help, you will have a place to put the information you receive. Once you know what you think, you are in the best place to end up satisfied by the answer you finally decide on.

The other assignment was to *Flicker Mark 10:13-16.*

> *Mark 10:13 And they were bringing children to Him so that He might touch them; but the disciples rebuked them.*
>
> *Mark 10:14 But when Jesus saw this, He was indignant and said to them, "Permit the children to come to Me; do not hinder them; for the kingdom of God belongs to such as these.*
>
> *Mark 10:15 "Truly I say to you, whoever does not receive the kingdom of God like a child will not enter it [at] [all.]"*
>
> *Mark 10:16 And He took them in His arms and [began] blessing them, laying His hands on them. (NASB)*

This passage is similar to another passage we studied earlier that also uses the analogy of a child and the kingdom, *Matthew 18:1-4.* This one is slightly different. But the repetition of multiple stories all pointing to the virtue of child-like attitudes underscore how important this must be to God.

I wonder why it is so hard for us to have child-like faith in Jesus as our loving parent and protector? That is what He wants. Plus, I'll bet if we were in His position, that is probably what we would want too.

Flicker Practice

Flicker the short verses on the following pages. Write your answers in the provided *FLCR* panels.

If you get stuck you can check the Appendix titled *Answers* for some ideas.

1 John 3:16 We know love by this, that He laid down His life for us; and we ought to lay down our lives for the brethren. (NASB)

Lessons

Challenges

Responses

John 15:7 "If you abide in Me, and My words abide in you, ask whatever you wish, and it will be done for you. (NASB)

Lessons

Challenges

Responses

About Flicker Practice

A question that comes up about *Flickering* Bible passages during your Time with God is how long each passage should be. Passages that are telling a narrative story can generally be longer than logical material like *Romans*.

But the rule of thumb is to read and write *Facts* down about the passage until one or two *verses* strike you. Then dig in and do all the *FLCR* steps on those verses. The next day, start where you left off and do the same.

Another question that comes up is how to *Flicker* Bible passages that are in a read-through-the-Bible schedule. The problem is that most of those schedules call for more verses to be read each day than can comfortably be *Flickered* by most people.

These programs are good for getting a sense of the whole Bible and you can use *Flicker* to go through them, but I would suggest you use the following approach to do so.

Since there is too much material, the trick is to lightly look through the passage(s) for today looking for something you would like to read and *Flicker*. This should take no more than five minutes. But wait, you say. You are not a good reader and sometimes they call for several chapters on a given day. How can you read all that in five minutes. Because I am suggesting that you *not* read the chapters. Instead, just look through them for something to read. This process is known as skimming the verses and it does an excellent job of giving you an overall exposure to large portions of the Bible.

Give it a try. Take five minutes and look from beginning to end of today's chapters and look for something that is about two to four verses long and read and *Flicker* those verses.

Assignment 7

Motivation

1. Do I want to know God?

2. How do I want my life to be?

3. Do I want to do His will for my life?

4. Do I want to please God?

5. Do I want to know His heart and what He cares about?

6. Would I prefer my independence over His will and way?

7. It might change my priorities. What do I really want?

Continue to ponder these seven questions and the three verses: *Ephesians 3:16-19, Matthew 12:30-31*, and *Luke 18:13*. Explore the questions you hesitate on and see if you can untangle what is holding you back.

Skill

Flicker Luke 8:22-25. Write out the *Facts, Lessons, Challenges,* and *Responses* in the *FLCR* panels provided on the next couple of pages.

Also, read the Appendix titled *Designing a Time with God*. This gives you some fresh thoughts about how to match your activities to your current interests and level of *Desire*.

If you get stuck on *Luke 8:22-25* you can check the Appendix titled *Answers* for some ideas.

Luke 8:22 Now on one of [those] days Jesus and His disciples got into a boat, and He said to them, "Let us go over to the other side of the lake." So they launched out.

Luke 8:23 But as they were sailing along He fell asleep; and a fierce gale of wind descended on the lake, and they [began] to be swamped and to be in danger.

Luke 8:24 They came to Jesus and woke Him up, saying, "Master, Master, we are perishing!" And He got up and rebuked the wind and the surging waves, and they stopped, and it became calm.

Luke 8:25 And He said to them, "Where is your faith?" They were fearful and amazed, saying to one another, "Who then is this, that He commands even the winds and the water, and they obey Him?" (NASB)

Lessons

Challenges

Responses

"If you enjoy
your time with God,
you will do it again.
And if you
keep showing up,
God will change you."

The Authors

Chapter 8
Pacing Your Growth

"We want you to carry these bricks around and stack them where the workers can easily get them."

The task did not seem very hard. All I [N] had to do is move some bricks. It was the first day of my summer job in college and I was hired to be an architect's assistant. The first day they had me working at the construction site.

What struck me about the workers at the site was how slowly they were working. I was young and strong and set out to move the flat of bricks with skill and determination.

The first 10 loads went fine. Then each load seemed to get heaver. I was determined to make good on my commitment so I redoubled my effort. But with each load, my loathing of bricks increased. By the end of the day I never wanted to see another brick. The other workers had not skipped a beat, accomplished a lot, and had great attitudes about their work.

My eagerness to do a good job had persuaded me to take a pace that was too ambitious, and ended up ruining the job for me. It would have been better to take a slower pace, like the other workers, and go for effectiveness over a longer period of time.

When you begin having a Time with God, it can be very tempting to commit to an overly ambitious schedule. It is important to remember that lasting change happens gradually over time.

Denise's testimony is an excellent example how a modest pace can enable long-term growth.

Review Motivation Assignment 7

But before we look at Denise's testimony, we'll have one last review of your process of uncovering your Desire to know God.

1. Do I want to know God?

2. How do I want my life to be?

3. Do I want to do His will for my life?

4. Do I want to please God?

5. Do I want to know His heart and what He cares about?

6. Would I prefer my independence over His will and way?

7. It might change my priorities. What do I really want?

If the question you hesitate on is question 7 above, *Family of Origin Issues (FOOI)* may be at work.

FOOI can keep you in a defensive position in life. As a child you might have grown up only responding to what is asked of you. You don't have the resources to take the lead and get an offense. You just defend against life.

As a child, if you didn't understand what would satisfy the authorities in your life, it would be difficult for you to trust them and would leave you always reacting to life and never taking charge of it.

If this was your background, when you become an adult and actually can take the lead in your life you probably wouldn't feel confident enough to take an offense in life. It is too unfamiliar. Just like you didn't know what would satisfy the authorities as a child, now you are not sure what would satisfy you, what you want. You worry you will make things worse. You choose to just react instead of getting out in front of life, trusting your judgment, making a plan, and making your life about your values and choices.

A life that is only defensive and only in reaction can begin to kill your soul. The first step to getting an offense in life is to write out how you want your life to be as a child of God.

Testimony

When I [D] was saved, I developed a very simple Time with God using a small devotional pamphlet that I enjoyed and my walk with God was going along nicely.

Then after a few years I found myself in a complex course in Methodical Bible Study as part of my undergraduate work. Unfortunately, it was not a very good course and by the end of it I wound up hating Bible study.

After the course, I found myself in no man's land. I did not like the new Bible study methods, but did not feel I could go back to my small devotional pamphlet since I knew all the new methods. So I did nothing for several years.

Then I came across 1 *Peter 2:2,*

> 1 Peter 2:2 **Like a newborn baby, crave pure spiritual milk**, *so that by it you may grow up in your salvation,… (NIV1984)*

This verse challenged my life. I had just delivered our first child and I did not want to be the kind of mother that just went to church on Sunday but never opened her Bible at home. This verse said I had a *Desire* for Bible study that was just as natural as a baby's *Desire* for milk. I remembered having that *Desire* when I first came to Christ. So I set out to resurface the *Desire* God gave me to be with Him.

For a few months I would stop for about 5 minutes each day and ponder the same questions you have on your reminder card (cf. page 236). Eventually I felt my desire beginning to surface.

Then I wanted to design a Time with God that would feed my *Desire* without overwhelming it. What intrigued me was to learn what God is like. So, I decided to start reading in Genesis and read through the Bible noticing what God did, what He valued, what He enjoyed, and what concerned Him. Sometimes I would read 1 or 2 verses and find something about Him. Other times I would need to read many verses. But I found this approach appealed to me and did not overwhelm my *Desire*.

At this point in my life, I decided my *Desire* could support three sessions per week on Monday, Wednesday, and Friday. Noon time was the best time for me. That was when I put my daughter down to sleep and I had the right kind of energy.

Through trial and error I had to figure out how to guard this dedicated time. I had been having my Time with God about two weeks when a girlfriend called to ask me if I could baby-sit her newborn while she went to the doctor. I said "sure." I fed my baby and her's and put them down for a nap so I could have my Time with God.

My daughter went to sleep, but her daughter started screaming. She was fed and dry and I feared there was no cure for her gas. I paced back and forth with her, to no avail. I reminded God that this was my time to meet with Him and that I *really* wanted to meet with Him, but if she continued to wail I would miss out.

I will never forget what happened next. All of a sudden there was *quiet*. I looked down and she was sleeping peacefully in my arms. A few seconds ago she had been beet red with veins popping out of her forehead. Now she was peaches and cream. A few seconds ago her face had been wet with tears. Now she was dry with one little tear drop in the corner of her eye. I would have expected her breathing to be ragged and shallow from all the screaming, but she was peaceful and silent. I put her down and had a wonderful Time with God.

The next week, my friend asked if I could baby-sit again. I said "No problem." Once again I put both babies down for their nap so I could have my Time with God. Once again her baby began to wail. I prayed the same prayer, but this time to no avail. I felt like God was telling me, "You say your Time with Me is a priority, but what are you doing to protect it?" I had to suffer through the colic and miss my Time with God that day. Protecting my Time with God became my priority. No more baby-sitting Monday, Wednesday or Friday at noon. I was responsible to keep my chosen time viable.

I kept my Time with God at three sessions per week for 20 years while we raised our four children. During that time it grew from 15 to 30 minutes, then to 60 minutes, then to 90 minutes per session. It is amazing what you can accomplish three times per week if you keep showing up. When my last child left for college, my *Desire* had grown to the point that I was more than ready to go to seven sessions per week. Now, if I miss a session it feels like I have missed a nourishing meal and I will try and fit it in some way.

Something else has happened over the years. When I first started, my *Desire* was easily shaken so the choice of time was very important. It needed to be in a good time. Now, my *Desire* has developed so that I can have an effective Time with God in a range of time slots. But most of the time I still keep it in my ideal time of day.

It truly is amazing how your relationship with God can grow just dedicating a few days a week to meet with Him. Your understanding of who He is, how He leads and what He cares about all come into clearer focus. Dedicating three days a week for 20 years transformed my life. It was a modest investment for such a big payoff.

God Loves Small Beginnings

Often it takes humility to admit the true level of your *Desire* for God and start there. There is a temptation to worry that you should be further along. But keep in mind that our walk with God is not about us—our performance or our power.

> 1. To admit the true level of your *Desire*, often it takes
>
> _____

In *Ephesians 3:16-18* God makes it clear that it is all about God and His love for us. It is not about us.

> *Ephesians 3:16-18 I pray that out of **his** glorious riches **he** may strengthen you with power **through his Spirit** in your inner being, so that Christ may dwell in your hearts through **faith**. And I pray that you, being rooted and established **in love**, may have **power**, together with all the saints, to grasp how wide and long and high and deep is the **love of Christ**, (NIV1984)*

Remember how you received Christ? In *Colossians 2:6* the Bible says we are to continue our walk with Christ the same way we began our walk with Christ.

> *Colossians 2:6 So then, **just as** you received Christ Jesus as Lord, **continue** to live in him, rooted and built up in him, strengthened in the **faith** as you were taught, and overflowing with **thankfulness**. (NIV1984)*

We received Christ in faith and thankfulness. When we received Christ, God gave us a love for Him. The Christian walk is not about us but it is about Him and the love He gave us for Him. In *Revelation 2:4* the Bible reminds us to not forsake this first love.

> *Revelation 2:4 Yet I hold this against you: You have forsaken your **first love**. (NIV1984)*

God is reasonable. He is clear. He is asking us to put our effort into knowing and loving Him. The focus is on God and He is 100% OK with small beginnings.

2. God is 100% OK with

_____

In *Mark 4:30-32* Jesus used the example of the mustard seed to illustrate spiritual growth. The mustard seed was the smallest cultivated seed in Jesus' day. It was 1/20 of an inch—a pinhead. It has remarkable growth. The plant grows 10-12 feet high and the stem is the size of a man's arm.

> *Mark 4:30-32 Again he said, "What shall we say **the kingdom of God is like**, or what parable shall we use to describe it? **It is like a mustard seed, which is the smallest seed** you plant in the ground. Yet when planted, it grows and becomes the largest of all garden plants, with such big branches that the birds of the air can perch in its shade." (NIV1984)*

God loves small beginnings. He created many nations with one man Abraham. He offered salvation to all through one Savior Jesus Christ. He propelled one roomful of disciples to change the world. God loves to honor small faith in simple truth.

Find the level of your *Desire*. Then be humble enough to start there. God has provided us with the *Desire* for Him and His word. If we nourish our *Desire* and lead with it, His word can *Transform* us.

Review Skill Assignment 7

One of the *Skill* assignments was to read the Appendix titled *Designing a Time with God*. As you think about creating a Time with God that works for you, begin with an accurate sense for how strong your current *Desire* to know God is and design something that meets you where you are. If you design something that is too taxing, you will smother your *Desire*. If it is too easy, you will be bored and lose interest. Your design should match your current level of *Desire*.

The other assignment was to *Flicker Luke 8:22-25*.

> *Luke 8:22 Now on one of [those] days Jesus and His disciples got into a boat, and He said to them, "Let us go over to the other side of the lake." So they launched out.*
>
> *Luke 8:23 But as they were sailing along He fell asleep; and a fierce gale of wind descended on the lake, and they [began] to be swamped and to be in danger.*
>
> *Luke 8:24 They came to Jesus and woke Him up, saying, "Master, Master, we are perishing!" And He got up and rebuked the wind and the surging waves, and they stopped, and it became calm.*
>
> *Luke 8:25 And He said to them, "Where is your faith?" They were fearful and amazed, saying to one another, "Who then is this, that He commands even the winds and the water, and they obey Him?"* (NASB)

After you gathered your *Facts* for this passage and were looking for *Lessons*, what stood out as unusual to you? From where I [N] sit there are two unusual things: 1) that the wind and waves obeyed Jesus and 2) that His greatest concern was the disciples' lack of faith.

The first unusual thing could be stated as a *Lesson* like this, "Jesus is in control of the physical world we live in." Turning it into a *Challenge* we have, "Am I willing to view the natural functioning of the world around me (the wind, the clouds, the sunsets) as under the control of the One I serve rather than just random events?"

What is unusual about the second thing is that it seems normal to me that the disciples would be frightened for their life. Yet Jesus' concern implies if they were trusting Him they wouldn't have been so panicked. From this unusual thing we could form the *Lesson,* "When we encounter frightening times, we should remember that He is ultimately in charge of them and should trust Him for the outcome." Turning that into a *Challenge,* "When I encounter frightening times, am I willing to remember that ultimately he is in control and is with me through this?"

Flicker Practice

Flicker the short verses on the following pages. Write your answers in the provided *FLCR* panels.

If you get stuck you can check the Appendix titled *Answers* for some ideas.

Proverbs 16:24

Facts

Proverbs 16:24 Pleasant words are a honeycomb, Sweet to the soul and healing to the bones. (NASB)

Lessons

Challenges

Responses

Proverbs 15:1 A gentle answer turns away wrath, But a harsh word stirs up anger. (NASB)

Lessons

Challenges

Responses

About Flicker Practice

These two verses represent a new kind of Bible literature for us. Our previous passages have been either logical literature like *Ephesians* or *Romans* that state what is right or wrong or narrative literature like *Matthew* or *Mark* that convey the truth in story form.

These verses are taken from wisdom literature which is also usually poetic literature.

The book of Psalms is the best example of poetic literature. Poetry makes strong use of figures of speech like "pearls of wisdom" or "go to the ant thou sluggard." Poetry uses words like "pearls" or "ant" as figures to represent something like "high value" or "tireless industry." Don't try and press the figure of speech and need to know exactly which type of "pearl" or "ant" is being referenced. Instead enjoy the beauty of this kind of indirect expression.

Wisdom literature is in books like *Proverbs, Song of Songs,* and *Ecclesiastes.* What is special about this is that is gives principles rather than promises. It describes how things usually work out rather than guarantee how they will work out.

For example, *Proverbs 16:24* says that "pleasant words" are healing to the recipient. It is saying that things generally get better in the presence of "pleasant words." But it is not a promise that somebody will always be healed if you speak "pleasant words" to them. In the same way in *Proverbs 15:1* "a gentle answer" usually "turns away wrath." But a person may be bound and determined to be angry. In that case "a gentle answer" won't force them to be happy.

As you look for your *Lessons* in poetic wisdom literature keep in mind that it uses figures of speech to set forth principles that are generally true.

Conclusion

Keep adjusting your Time with God so you can keep enjoying it. If you enjoy it, you will do it again. And if you keep showing up, God will change you.

> 3. If you enjoy it, you will
>
> _____
>
> 4. And if you keep showing up, God will
>
> _____

God has given us a chance to hunger and thirst for Him. Will you *Desire* that and set your mind on it? Will you pray diligently for that?

Where is your focus? In *Joshua 24:15* God challenges us to face where we are putting our focus.

> *Joshua 24:15 "But if serving the Lord seems undesirable to you, then choose for yourselves this day whom you will serve." (NIV1984)*

Get to know God. He is the answer. Find how you like to spend time with Him and do that. Find when you like to spend time with Him and do it then. God will fill your emptiness, and change your life.

May God bless you.

Appendix

"If you have faith
the size of a mustard seed,
you will say to this mountain,
'Move from here to there,'
and it will move;
and nothing will be
impossible to you."

Matthew 17:20 (NASB)

When you pray, align yourself with what God has promised to do. These pages contain many of God's promises and are organized by category. When you have a need, find a promise that addresses your need, then tell God you are trusting Him to meet keep His promise in the area of your need. Instead of praying the problems, pray the promises (cf. page 168).

Guidance

Psalms 37:23 The steps of a man are established by the LORD, And He delights in his way. (NASB)

Psalms 48:14 For such is God, Our God forever and ever; He will guide us until death. (NASB)

Psalms 73:24 With Your counsel You will guide me, And afterward receive me to glory. (NASB)

Proverbs 3:6 In all your ways acknowledge Him, And He will make your paths straight. (NASB)

Proverbs 16:9 The mind of man plans his way, But the LORD directs his steps. (NASB)

Isaiah 30:21 Your ears will hear a word behind you, "This is the way, walk in it," whenever you turn to the right or to the left. (NASB)

Isaiah 58:11 "And the LORD will continually guide you, And satisfy your desire in scorched places, And give strength to your bones; And you will be like a watered garden, And like a spring of water whose waters do not fail." (NASB)

Forgiveness

Psalms 32:5 I acknowledged my sin to You, And my iniquity I did not hide; I said, "I will confess my transgressions to the LORD"; And You forgave the guilt of my sin. Selah. (NASB)

Psalms 103:12 As far as the east is from the west, So far has He removed our transgressions from us. (NASB)

1 John 1:9 If we confess our sins, He is faithful and righteous to forgive us our sins and to cleanse us from all unrighteousness. (NASB)

Sickness

Exodus 15:26 And He said, "If you will give earnest heed to the voice of the LORD your God, and do what is right in His sight, and give ear to His commandments, and keep all His statutes, I will put none of the diseases on you which I have put on the Egyptians; for I, the LORD, am your healer." (NASB)

Exodus 23:25 "But you shall serve the LORD your God, and He will bless your bread and your water; and I will remove sickness from your midst." (NASB)

Deuteronomy 7:15 "The LORD will remove from you all sickness; and He will not put on you any of the harmful diseases of Egypt which you have known, but He will lay them on all who hate you." (NASB)

Psalms 41:3 The LORD will sustain him upon his sickbed; In his illness, You restore him to health. (NASB)

Psalms 103:3 Who pardons all your iniquities, Who heals all your diseases; (NASB)

Proverbs 4:20,22 My son, give attention to my words; incline your ear to my sayings. For they are life to those who find the and health to all their body. (NASB)

James 5:14 Is anyone among you sick? [Then] he must call for the elders of the church and they are to pray over him, anointing him with oil in the name of the Lord; (NASB)

Trouble

Psalms 18:2 The LORD is my rock and my fortress and my deliverer, My God, my rock, in whom I take refuge; My shield and the horn of my salvation, my stronghold. (NASB)

Psalms 22:24 For He has not despised nor abhorred the affliction of the afflicted; Nor has He hidden His face from him; But when he cried to Him for help, He heard. (NASB)

Psalms 34:19 Many are the afflictions of the righteous, But the LORD delivers him out of them all. (NASB)

Psalms 55:22 Cast your burden upon the LORD and He will sustain you; He will never allow the righteous to be shaken. (NASB)

Psalms 107:19 Then they cried out to the LORD in their trouble; He saved them out of their distresses. (NASB)

Psalms 145:14 The LORD sustains all who fall And raises up all who are bowed down. (NASB)

Proverbs 11:8 The righteous is delivered from trouble, But the wicked takes his place. (NASB)

Proverbs 24:16 For a righteous man falls seven times, and rises again, But the wicked stumble in [time of] calamity. (NASB)

Jeremiah 29:11 'For I know the plans that I have for you,' declares the LORD, 'plans for welfare and not for calamity to give you a future and a hope. (NASB)

Marriage

Proverbs 12:4 An excellent wife is the crown of her husband, But she who shames [him] is like rottenness in his bones. (NASB)

Proverbs 12:7 The wicked are overthrown and are no more, But the house of the righteous will stand. (NASB)

Mark 10:7-9 "FOR THIS REASON A MAN SHALL LEAVE HIS FATHER AND MOTHER AND THE TWO SHALL BECOME ONE FLESH; so they are no longer two, but one flesh. "What therefore God has joined together, let no man separate." (NASB)

Ephesians 5:22 Wives, [be subject] to your own husbands, as to the Lord. (NASB)

Ephesians 5:25 Husbands, love your wives, just as Christ also loved the church and gave Himself up for her (NASB)

Ephesians 5:28 So husbands ought also to love their own wives as their own bodies. He who loves his own wife loves himself (NASB)

Colossians 3:18-19 Wives, be subject to your husbands, as is fitting in the Lord. Husbands, love your wives and do not be embittered against them. (NASB)

Hebrews 13:4 Marriage [is to be held] in honor among all, and the [marriage] bed [is to be] undefiled; for fornicators and adulterers God will judge. (NASB)

Titus 2:2-6 Older men are to be temperate, dignified, sensible, sound in faith, in love, in perseverance. Older women likewise are to be reverent in their behavior, not malicious gossips nor enslaved to much wine, teaching what is good, so that they may encourage the young women to love their husbands, to love their children, [to be] sensible, pure, workers at home, kind, being subject to their own husbands, so that the word of God will not be dishonored. Likewise urge the young men to be sensible (NASB)

1 Peter 3:1-7 In the same way, you wives, be submissive to your own husbands so that even if any [of them] are disobedient to the word, they may be won without a word by the behavior of their wives, as they observe your chaste and respectful behavior. Your adornment must not be [merely] external—braiding the hair, and wearing gold jewelry, or putting on dresses; but [let it be] the hidden person of the heart, with the imperishable quality of a gentle and quiet spirit, which is precious in the sight of God. For in this way in former times the holy women also, who hoped in God, used to adorn themselves, being submissive to their own husbands; just as Sarah obeyed Abraham, calling him lord, and you have become her children if you do what is right without being frightened by any fear. You husbands in the same way, live with [your wives] in an understanding way, as with someone weaker, since she is a woman; and show her honor as a fellow heir of the grace of life, so that your prayers will not be hindered. (NASB)

1 Peter 3:8-11 To sum up, all of you be harmonious, sympathetic, brotherly, kindhearted, and humble in spirit; not returning evil for evil or insult for insult, but giving a blessing instead; for you were called for the very purpose that you might inherit a blessing. For, "THE ONE WHO DESIRES LIFE, TO LOVE AND SEE GOOD DAYS, MUST KEEP HIS TONGUE FROM EVIL AND HIS LIPS FROM SPEAKING DECEIT. "HE MUST TURN AWAY FROM EVIL AND DO GOOD; HE MUST SEEK PEACE AND PURSUE IT. (NASB)

Children

Deuteronomy 4:40 "So you shall keep His statutes and His commandments which I am giving you today, that it may go well with you and with your children after you, and that you may live long on the land which the LORD your God is giving you for all time." (NASB)

Deuteronomy 5:29 'Oh that they had such a heart in them, that they would fear Me and keep all My commandments always, that it may be well with them and with their sons forever! (NASB)

Psalms 37:25 I have been young and now I am old, Yet I have not seen the righteous forsaken Or his descendants begging bread. (NASB)

Proverbs 11:21 Assuredly, the evil man will not go unpunished, But the descendants of the righteous will be delivered. (NASB)

Proverbs 14:26 In the fear of the LORD there is strong confidence, And his children will have refuge. (NASB)

Proverbs 20:7 A righteous man who walks in his integrity — How blessed are his sons after him. (NASB)

Jeremiah 32:39 and I will give them one heart and one way, that they may fear Me always, for their own good and for [the good of] their children after them. (NASB)

Safety

Psalms 16:8 I have set the LORD continually before me; Because He is at my right hand, I will not be shaken. (NASB)

Psalms 27:1 The LORD is my light and my salvation; Whom shall I fear? The LORD is the defense of my life; Whom shall I dread? (NASB)

Psalms 121:1-3 I will lift up my eyes to the mountains; From where shall my help come? My help [comes] from the LORD, Who made heaven and earth. He will not allow your foot to slip; He who keeps you will not slumber. (NASB)

Proverbs 1:33 "But he who listens to me shall live securely And will be at ease from the dread of evil." (NASB)

Proverbs 18:10 The name of the LORD is a strong tower; The righteous runs into it and is safe. (NASB)

Need for Success or Prosperity

Deuteronomy 28:11 "The LORD will make you abound in prosperity, in the offspring of your body and in the offspring of your beast and in the produce of your ground, in the land which the LORD swore to your fathers to give you." (NASB)

Psalms 1:3 He will be like a tree [firmly] planted by streams of water, Which yields its fruit in its season And its leaf does not wither; And in whatever he does, he prospers. (NASB)

Psalms 57:2 I will cry to God Most High, To God who accomplishes [all things] for me. (NASB)

Proverbs 8:18 "Riches and honor are with me [wisdom], Enduring wealth and righteousness." (NASB)

Proverbs 10:22 It is the blessing of the LORD that makes rich, And He adds no sorrow to it. (NASB)

Proverbs 15:6 Great wealth is [in] the house of the righteous, But trouble is in the income of the wicked. (NASB)

Joel 2:26 "You will have plenty to eat and be satisfied And praise the name of the LORD your God, Who has dealt wondrously with you; Then My people will never be put to shame." (NASB)

Matthew 6:25-26 "For this reason I say to you, do not be worried about your life, [as to] what you will eat or what you will drink; nor for your body, [as to] what you will put on. Is not life more than food, and the body more than clothing? Look at the birds of the air, that they do not sow, nor reap nor gather into barns, and [yet] your heavenly Father feeds them. Are you not worth much more than they?" (NASB)

Matthew 6:30-33 "But if God so clothes the grass of the field, which is [alive] today and tomorrow is thrown into the furnace, [will He] not much more [clothe] you? You of little faith! Do not worry then, saying, 'What will we eat?' or 'What will we drink?' or 'What will we wear for clothing?' For the Gentiles eagerly seek all these things; for your heavenly Father knows that you need all these things. But seek first His kingdom and His righteousness, and all these things will be added to you. (NASB)

Philippians 4:19 And my God will supply all your needs according to His riches in glory in Christ Jesus. (NASB)

God Keeps His Promises

Numbers 23:19 "God is not a man, that He should lie, Nor a son of man, that He should repent; Has He said, and will He not do it? Or has He spoken, and will He not make it good? (NASB)

Joshua 23:14 "Now behold, today I am going the way of all the earth, and you know in all your hearts and in all your souls that not one word of all the good words which the LORD your God spoke concerning you has failed; all have been fulfilled for you, not one of them has failed. (NASB)

1 Kings 8:56 "Blessed be the LORD, who has given rest to His people Israel, according to all that He promised; not one word has failed of all His good promise, which He promised through Moses His servant. (NASB)

Romans 4:21 and being fully assured that what God had promised, He was able also to perform. (NASB)

Hebrews 10:23 Let us hold fast the confession of our hope without wavering, for He who promised is faithful; (NASB)

"The LORD'S
lovingkindnesses
indeed never cease,
For His compassions
never fail."

Lamentations 3:22 (NASB)

1 Chapter

Desire-led or Discipline-led?

1.   Desire-led   Discipline-led

Skill Time: Learning to See

2.   See

Video Clip

- Four guys sitting on a road.
- They are not busy.
- They don't have much to do.
- They are about to graduate.
- Then they are leaving town together.
- Three of them are in shorts.
- They are sitting in front of an old run down gas station.
- The leader of the group socially seems to be the third guy.
- All four of them are graduating.

Bible Passage *(Mark 12:41-44)*

- Jesus sat down by the treasury.
- He was watching how people were putting money into the treasury.
- Many rich people put in large sums.
- A poor widow put in a small amount.
- She probably felt embarrassed about how little she gave in comparison.
- Jesus said she gave more than the other contributors.
- They gave out of their surplus but she gave all she had.

1 Assignment—Mark 6:1-4

Facts

- Jesus came to His own hometown.
- Jesus began to teach in the synagogue.
- People were surprised He was so wise and could do such miracles.
- They took offense because they remembered the way He was when He was growing up with His brothers and sisters.
- A prophet does not have honor in his hometown with his relatives and childhood friends.

2 Chapter

Desire Squasher: Deceitful Desires

1. To lie "
2. Does not deliver
3. The path to God
4. Fulfillment   Numb you
5. From God
6. Grow

What Do You Want?

7. Hesitating
8. Effort

FLCR—Facts

9. See
10. Withhold judgement
11. See
12. God told him to go without telling him where to go

FLCR—Lessons

13. Learned
14. Unusual to you
15. Learn something from it
16. Sometimes God asks us to take action before we have all the necessary information

FLCR—Challenges

17. My life
18. Lessons
19. Am I willing to take action before I have all the necessary information?

FLCR—Responses

20. Respond to God
21. Father, I know you value trust. When you want me to take action, help me to trust you enough to take action.

2 Practice—John 11:35

Facts

- It is talking about Jesus.
- It is saying that Jesus wept.

Lessons

- Jesus has feelings.
- Jesus knows what it is like to be sad to the point of tears.

Challenges

- When I pray to God am I willing to approach Him like He has feelings?

- Do I believe that Jesus knows what it feels like to be sad to the point of tears?

Responses

- Father, thank you for being someone who can relate to how I feel.
- Thank you for being vulnerable to let me know that You feel hurt sometimes.

2 Practice—Psalm 34:19

Facts

- The people of God have many afflictions.
- God does not keep His people from difficulties.
- God delivers His people from difficulties.
- God delivers His people from each and every difficulty.

Lessons

- Affliction is more the norm for the people of God rather than the exception.
- God is actively engaged in delivering His people from every affliction.

Challenges

- Am I OK with affliction being a normal part of my life, knowing that God will deliver me from every one of them?
- Can I believe God is engaged and actively delivering me from my current affliction(s) even when I can not see it?

Responses

- Father, I thank You that walking with You is not fragile and that You are at work on my behalf to deliver me from the difficulties I am facing.
- I love it when You said, "out of them all."
- Thank You for Your work on my behalf.

2 Practice—Psalm 19:1

Facts

- He is saying something about the sky ("the heavens").
- Somehow the sky is telling me something about God.
- The sky helps me understand something about how great God is.
- The sky is God's handiwork for us to admire and learn from.

Lessons

- God is vast and magnificent, virtually limitless.
- God is an artist and appreciates beauty (as seen in a beautiful sunset). He is also very powerful (as seen in a massive storm).

Challenges

- When I look at the sky, do I see how much God is bigger than my problems?
- When I see a beautiful sunset or an intense storm, do I pause and take in what God is telling me about Himself?

Responses

- Father, You are great and glorious.
- Thank You for reminding me to not view my problems as being so big in comparison with what You are like and with what it is like to be in Your presence.

2 Assignment—Hebrews 11:8-11

Facts

- He obeyed God's call even though he did not know where he was going.
- He used faith while he lived in tents as an alien.
- Sarah considered God faithful to keep His promise to have her conceive beyond the proper time.

Lessons

- Obeying and following God requires a life of faith because it won't always make sense.
- God's direction can feel unnatural and makeshift.
- God is faithful to keep His promises.
- God values faith, obedience, and adventure.

Challenges

- Have I responded in faith to God's leading?
- How do I gip myself of God's inheritance?
- Do I expect God's will to be clear, risk-free, and comfortable?
- Do I value faith, trust, obedience, and adventure?

Responses

- Please help me to have the faith, trust, obedience and sense of adventure I need to have to fully follow You.

3 Chapter

How We Think Effects How We Feel

1. The alarm clock rings   Cookie

How We Think Effects How We Grow

2. Transform us
3. Away from God
4. Transform us
5. Mind transplant
6. From God's point of view
7. Thoughts disobedient to Christ

Desire Squasher: Futile Thinking

8. Futile Thinking
9. Nowhere

Help with Finding the Lessons

10. Lessons

11. Video Clip

- If you are going to have a wedding by the water, don't stand so close to the water.
- .If you are going to be in the wedding party, practice walking the path you will be taking noticing any potential places you might trip.

3 Flicker Practice—Romans 5:8

Facts

- He is talking about how God demonstrates His love for us.
- He is saying that God showed his love by having Christ die for us.
- He is also saying that He did not wait until we were acting right or until we were deserving, but He showed His love while we were sinners.

Lessons

- God is different than man. He shows His love for us while we are behaving sinfully. We tend to show love only to those who deserve it.
- Showing love can be painful. Christ showed His love for us by dying for us while we were behaving sinfully.

Challenges

- Am I willing to show love to those who are still mistreating me?
- Am I willing to show love if it is painful or costly?

Response

- Father, thank You for being willing to demonstrate Your love for me while I was a sinner.
- Thank You for sacrificing Your only Son for me.
- Thank You for being willing to suffer on my behalf.
- Please help me to be like You.
- I want to understand how to show love to those who are behaving badly without becoming a door mat.
- Please help me to be loving and yet wise like You.

3 Assignment—Genesis 12:1-5

Facts

- God promised:
- Make him into great nation
- Bless him
- Make his name great
- He will be a blessing
- Bless those who bless him
- Curse those who curse him
- The whole earth will be blessed by him
- Abraham obeyed and left
- Lot and Sarai went
- They took all their possessions

- They took hired help
- They set out for Canaan
- Made it to destination

Lessons

- God asked him to leave his family, country, but allowed him to take his possessions. God did not mind him having things. He wanted Abraham to trust Him.
- God shares HIs glory and greatness—He made Abraham's name great.
- God reveals His will gradually
- God showed him the way
- God blesses those follow HIm
- We can get blessings by blessing those close to God
- We can get cursed by hurting those close to God
- God uses us even in later life

Challenges

- Do I need to step out in my writing or teaching?
- Do I trust God to show me the way?
- Do I expect God to use me as I get older?

Responses

- Please help me stay close and follow You my whole life.
- I want to glorify You even in old age.

4 Chapter

Independence from God

1. Independence from God
2. God's mercy

God's Help

3. Took   Blessed   Broke   Gave

Desire Squasher: Taking Offense

4. Deceitful Desires   Futile Thinking   Taking Offense
5. All the information   Take that thought captive

4 Flicker Practice—Philippians 2:4

Facts

- He is talking about my things. My own personal interests.
- He is also talking about the things or interests of others.
- He is talking about what I should give attention to.
- He is saying I should not just be interested in my things, I should also look out for the things of others.

Lessons

- I should not just be focused on what I need. I should also look out for what other people need.

- I am not an island. God created us to watch out for and help one another as needs arise.

Challenges

- Am I willing to take the time to listen to the needs of others (neighbors, small group members, etc.) and help out when I can?
- As much as I want to be successful myself, am I willing to divert some of that effort to help others to be successful?

Response

- Father, I see that you don't want my focus to be just on myself.
- Help me remember how You have made us to help each other.
- Today I am going to watch for the opportunity to help someone else.

4 Flicker Practice—Psalm 56:3-4

Facts

- This is about what to do when I am afraid.
- When the author is afraid, he puts his trust in God.
- The author determines to shift from fear to trust.
- He says that men do not have power over the author because the author is trusting in the One that created these men.

Lessons

- When I feel afraid, I should put my trust in God.
- God is more powerful than mere men.

Challenges

- Is there one situation today where I would be willing to exchange the fear of men for trust in God (knowing that God is more powerful than mere men).

Response

- Father I am happy to see your concern for me when I am fearful.
- I am happy to see that trust in You has power in this present life and in eternity with You.
- Help me find a situation today to exchange fear for trust in You and give me the courage to do it.

4 Assignment—Matthew 18:1-4

Facts

- The disciples want to know who is greatest in the kingdom of heaven.
- Jesus doesn't answer their question directly, but makes reference to a small child to answer it.
- Jesus says they need to become like little children to enter the kingdom of heaven.
- Children are humble, innocent, pure, simple, know their limitations, and easily believe what you tell them.

Lessons

- God measures greatness differently than we do. We think greatness is flashy, important, and powerful. God thinks greatness is simple humble-ness.
- God values our child-like characteristics like simplicity, innocence, belief, and humbleness.

Challenges

- When I look at a child, can I see what is "great" about child-like behavior?
- Can I get to a place where it makes sense to place more value on humble-ness than on accomplishments?

Response

- Father, it is so easy to get caught up on accomplishments and not focused on important character developments like the building of humility.
- Help me to value the character you are developing in me when I come upon obstacles and trouble, rather than focusing on the deadlines that are getting missed.

5 Chapter

Family of Origin Issues

1. You grew up in
2. 18 years old
3. Your job

Family of Origin Can Distort Bible Study

4. The Bible
5. Flaws

Get to Know God

6. Get to know God

Identify How God Differs From Your Parents

7. Of our parents

5 Flicker Practice—John 6:35

Facts

- Jesus is speaking.
- Jesus is bread of life.
- The one who comes to Jesus will never hunger.
- The one who believes in Jesus will never thirst.

Lessons

- Jesus is more nourishing to us spiritually than bread is to our bodies.
- To partake of Jesus' nourishment we need to come to Him and believe in Him.

Challenges

- Am I willing to turn to Him for comfort instead of food?
- Do I believe Jesus will help me if I come and believe in Him?

- Have I accepted the eternal life He offers and believed that His death on the cross makes my life possible by paying the penalty for my sins?

Response

- Father, You have the words of eternal life.
- I come and believe that You sent Jesus to save my soul from death and nourish me so I will never die, and live with you forever.
- Thank you for life and for bringing me to the living bread.

5 Flicker Practice—Psalm 139:14

Facts

- The author is giving back to God.
- He is thankful for God's care in creating him.
- When he thinks about what it must have taken to create him, he is gripped with respect and awe at how wonderfully he has been made.
- His soul is very aware that everything God does, He does wonderfully.

Lessons

- The mystifying and wonderful way we were created tells us how great God is.
- As one of HIs creations, we are examples of how well God does things.

Challenges

- Do I think of my body in all of its wonders as God's handiwork? Can I think of one way today to treat it as the special gift it is?
- When I get a cut or scrape and watch it heal, do I give God thanks for being a healer and healing me?

Response

- Father, You are so great! Your ways are so far beyond our understanding.
- You have designed and created our bodies full of ways to nourish, heal, and care for them.
- I am thankful for what You have done. Thank you for being my Healer.

5 Assignment—Philippians 1:9-11

Facts

- This passage is a prayer.
- He is talking about their love.
- He wants their love to increase.
- He wants their love to have more knowledge and discernment.
- He wants their love to become more discerning.
- "so that" identifies what will happen if our love increases.
- So that we will be blameless.
- He is talking about the results of living rightly.
- Our righteousness comes through Jesus Christ (Who must have loved with knowledge and discernment).

Lessons
- God wants our love to increase.
- God wants our love to be guided by real knowledge and discernment.
- We will be blameless if we increase our love with knowledge and discernment.

Challenges
- Am I willing to love more than I am right now?
- Am I willing to exercise some caution as I extend my love toward others?
- Do I believe I will be blameless if I exercise "smart" love?

Response
- Father, I marvel at the way you so freely extend Your love toward others, not based on their merits but based on Your giving nature.
- Help me keep in mind that when You love You are also exercising wisdom and discernment and help me do the same.

6 Chapter

Biblical Comfort Zone Examples
1. Comfort   Pleasure
2. Power

Introverts and Extroverts
3. Project
4. Introject
5. Responsibility   Word   Confess
6. Angry
7. Humility

Get to Know God
8. Compassionate
9. Comfort
10. Practice

6 Flicker Practice—Romans 8:31-32

Facts
- God is for us.
- Who can stand against us? God is more powerful than any created thing. If He is on our side, who can stand against Him?
- God is for us so much, He delivered His own Son for our benefit.
- If God is for us enough to give up His own Son, then He will also freely give us all things.

Lessons
- God is on our side.
- No one of significance can stand against us since God is on our side.
- God is on our side so much that He freely gives us Christ and all things.

Challenges

- Do I believe that the almighty God is on my side?
- After thinking of someone who stands against me, how would I say they compare to God (in strength, etc.)?
- Is there any greater way God could demonstrate that He is on our side?

Response

- Father, it is so easy to forget that You are on our side.
- And with You on our side all of our trouble fades by comparison.
- Thank you for giving me Christ and the other things I know about.
- But also thank you for giving me things I am not even aware of yet ("all things").

6 Flicker Practice—1 Peter 1:24-25

Facts

- He is talking about flesh and grass.
- He is comparing flesh with grass.
- He is comparing the glory of flesh to the flower of the grass.
- He is talking about how grass is temporary.
- He is saying that flesh is temporary like that.
- He is talking about the Word of the LORD.
- The Word of the LORD endures forever.
- He is contrasting something that withers with something that endures forever.
- Grass, flowers, and the flesh aspect of people wither and die.
- The thing that endures forever is the Word of the LORD.
- The Word of the LORD was preached to you.

Lessons

- Be aware that things of this life are temporary but the Word of the LORD endures forever.

Challenges

- Am I aware that everything around me is temporary and will wither?
- Do I put my trust in things around me or is my trust in the LORD?

Response

- Father, help me to see the temporariness of all that is around me.
- I love your Word. Help me center on it.
- Help me realize your Word will stand when everything else falls.

6 Assignment—Mark 10:13-16

Facts

- They are bringing children to Jesus.
- The disciples didn't like the idea.
- Jesus rebukes the disciples.

- Because the kingdom of God belongs to children.
- Everyone must be like a child to enter into the kingdom of God.
- Jesus brings the children close, blessing them and hugging them.

Lessons
- God values simple child-like faith.

Challenges
- Am I willing to unquestionably believe and follow God like a child would?

Response
- Thank you God that you made this so very simple.
- I pray that You would help me relate to You with child-like simplicity.

7 Chapter

Prayer in Three Steps
1. Align with God   Ask for what you want   Prepare to receive it
2. Anyone can do it

Step 1: Align with God
3. Connect with God
4. In Jesus name
5. He made it all possible
6. To give us
7. Bible prayers back to God
8. Resentment toward others
9. Judge and jury
10. To remain
11. Linger there
12. The most valuable thing in your life
13. Pleased
14. He has done for us
15. Visualization

Step 2: Ask for What You Want
16. Promises
17. Already promised to do
18. He can give
19. Hesitation
20. Our past experience
21. Stay connected
22. Joy is on the way
23. Accuracy
24. Receive your request

Step 3: Prepare to Receive It
25. Receive God's answer

26.   God's timing and provision

7 Flicker Practice—1 John 3:16

Facts

- We know love by this...
- That He laid down His life for us.
- We ought to lay down our lives for the brethren.

Lessons

- Christ demonstrated His love for us by dying for our sins.
- God wants us to have that kind of love for fellow believers.

Challenges

- Do take comfort in God's love for me because He died for me or do I need things to go smoothly in my life before I believe He loves me?
- His is my love for fellow believers?

Response

- Father, thank You for Your great sacrifice of love for me.
- Please forgive me when I am most assured of Your love when things are going well.
- Thank You for Your great example of love. Please help me to love my fellow believers like You do.

7 Flicker Practice—John 15:7

Facts

- He is saying if I abide in Him...
- And His words abide in me...
- I can ask for what I want and it will be done for me.

Lessons

- Abiding with God and filling our minds with His word unlocks two things: Our ability to ask for the right things and God's desire to give us whatever we ask for.
- God wants to answer our requests. He tells us how to pray so He can.

Challenges

- Am I abiding with God?
- Is my mind filled with God's word?
- Do I live like I believe God wants to answer my prayers?
- Am I willing to put effort toward abiding with God and with His word?

Response

- Father, You say if I abide in You and Your Words abide in me, I can ask for whatever I want and You will give it to me. Please help me cash this check.
- I want to abide in You.
- I love Your word. Please don't let me waste Your presence or Your word.
- I need Your help to be wise and put my effort into being with You.

- Please help me have a life spent with You.

7 Assignment—Luke 8:22-25

Facts

- Jesus and His disciples got into a boat and Jesus said, "Let's go across the lake."
- Jesus fell asleep as they sailed.
- A violent windstorm came.
- The boat started filling up with water to the point of danger.
- The disciples woke up Jesus calling Him "Master" and telling Him, "We are about to die."
- Jesus got up.
- Jesus rebuked the wind and raging waves.
- The waves and wind became calm.
- Jesus asked them, "Where is your faith?"
- The disciples were afraid and amazed wondering who Jesus really was since the winds and water obeyed Him.

Lessons

- Sometimes we should take Jesus at His word even if we are surrounded by the storms of life. If the disciples had taken Jesus at His word, they would have known they were going to get to the other side of the lake.
- Jesus wants our faith to be in Him, no matter what problems come up.
- Problems bigger than our ability to manage will come up as we follow Christ. The solution is our faith in Christ's ability to handle them.
- Jesus puts us before His own needs. He was tired, but He got up. He did not rebuke the disciples for interrupting His sleep. He taught them what would have been helpful for them in a crisis—faith.
- Satan is no match for Jesus. Satan might have been behind the storm trying to keep Jesus from getting to the demonized men at Gerasenes. Jesus was able to calm the storm by simply speaking a word.
- Jesus responds to our fears. He immediately calmed the storm. He did not play with their emotions.
- Jesus has ultimate control over His creation. His creation obeys His commands. When there are earthquakes, fires and floods, where is our faith?
- The disciples' lack of faith was more troubling to Jesus than the "dangerous" storm.

Challenges

- Am I taking God at His Word?
- Do I know that bigger problems than I can manage will come up as I follow Christ and that the solution is faith in Christ?
- Am I willing to follow Christ even when there is danger? Will my faith keep me focused on Him?
- Do I see how Christ will put me first? That He won't chastise me for being a bother to Him?
- Do I have faith that He will teach me what I need to increase my faith in order to manage a crisis?

- Do I rest in the idea that Satan is no match for God?
- Do I see how God cares about our fears? How He does not play with our emotions?
- Do I have faith that God has ultimate control over His creation?
- Where is my faith when there are earthquakes, fires, floods and tornados?
- When I am frightened, do I turn to God in faith?

Response
- Lord, please help me to trust Your leadership in my life.
- Please teach me how to follow You.
- Help me recognize the opportunities You give me and help me be brave enough to get in the boat with You.

8 Chapter

God Loves Small Beginnings
1.   Humility
2.   Small beginnings

Conclusion
10.   Do it again
11.   Change you

8 Flicker Practice—Proverbs 16:24

Facts
- Pleasant words are like honeycomb.
- Pleasant words are sweet to the soul.
- Pleasant words heal your bones.

Lessons
- We should not underestimate the power of pleasant words. They help our body and soul.

Challenges
- Do I realize the importance of pleasant words?
- Do I speak pleasantly?

Response
- Father, thank You for wanting us to speak pleasantly to one another.
- Thank You for the principle of healing when we are kind.
- Thank You for being such a kind Father.

8 Flicker Practice—Proverbs 15:1

Facts
- He is talking about how to reply to someone ("answer").
- He is contrasting two ways to respond to someone: with a gentle answer or with a harsh word.

- The 1st approach is careful, respectful, kind ("gentle").
- The 2nd approach is brash, unthinking, unrespectful ("harsh").
- The 1st approach has a soothing effect on the other person, calming someone who is ready to lash out in wrath ("turns away wrath").
- the 2nd approach tends to stir up a person to anger ("stirs up anger").

Lessons

- Your choice of the way you answer somebody can make your situation better or worse.
- A kind, gentle response tends to calm down an angry person.
- A harsh, unthinking response tends to agitate the person you are talking with.

Challenges

- Do I believe that my words play a large part in making my situation good or bad?
- Am I willing to keep my head when somebody comes at me with anger and respond with gentleness?
- When I feel like brushing someone off with a thoughtless brash response think about whether I am willing to manage their resulting anger.

Response

- Father, thank You that You reward thoughtfulness.
- Thank You that we have a significant influence on how others treat us.
- And thank You for telling us how to thrive.
- Give me the restraint to respond to people with gentle answers.

"Delight yourself
in the LORD;
and He will
give you
the desires
of your heart."

Psalm 34:4 (NASB)

"Set your mind on
the things above."

Colossians 3:2 (NASB)

Appendix C
Reminder Card

People who have taken the *How to Read the Bible So God Speaks to You* course have suggested that it would be helpful to have the seven questions described on page 39 and the three verses described on page 70 on a handy reminder card.

If the next two pages were cut out and placed on the front and back of a 4 x 6 index card they could become a convenient reminder card.

1. Do I want to know God?

2. How do I want my life to be?

3. Do I want to do His will for my life?

4. Do I want to please God?

5. Do I want to know His heart and what He cares about?

6. Would I prefer my independence over His will and way?

7. It might change my priorities. What do I really want?

And I pray that
you may have power to **grasp**

how **wide**
and **long**   is the
and **high**   **love**
and **deep**   of Christ

that you may be **filled**
to all the fullness of God

Eph 3:16-19 (NIV, subphrases omitted)

Love the Lord your God
with all your **heart**
and with all your **soul**
and with all your **mind**
and with all your **strength.**

Love your neighbor
as **yourself.**

Mark 12:30-31 (NIV, subphrases omitted)

God, have **mercy** on me,
a sinner.

Luke 18:13b (NIV)

"Take the leash
off your mind
and let it run freely."

Dr. Howard Hendricks

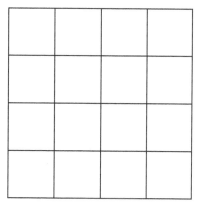

How many squares do you see above?

30 squares

As you look for squares,
look from different perspectives:
how many 4x4 squares,
how many 3x3 squares, etc.

Consider Bible passages
from different perspectives:
from the point of view of
different people in the passage,
for example.

Without lifting your pencil from the paper, draw four straight, connected lines which will go through each dot only once.

```
  •     •     •


  •     •     •


  •     •     •
```

The solution comes from going outside the 9 dots.

When looking at a Bible passage,
we tend to get stuck in one way of seeing it.
Move outside that grid and view the passage
in new ways and from new perspectives.

"If you can see it,
God can use it."

The Authors

"Your mind
never stops working.
Incubation invites
illumination."

Dr. Howard Hendricks

More Help with Finding the Lessons

As you *Flicker* a Bible passage, if you have difficulty coming up with the *Lessons*, here are some things you can try.

Clues

The first step in finding a *Lesson* in a difficult passage is to pretend that you are a detective and back off the idea of getting a *Lesson* in one step. Rather, start look for clues that might lead you to a *Lesson*.

One possible clue in the comic is the genuine attitude of repentance from the one apologizing. He really sounds like he is sorry. But the other person does not respond by softening his attitude. These clues guide you to look at what can be learned when a genuine apology is rejected.

In the *Passage 1* homework there are also clues. Did you notice that each verse starts out with the phrase "By faith?" If you treat this as a clue, you might want to consider how Abraham was having to use faith. What assurances was he having to do without as he obeyed God's voice. It is sometimes God's desire for us to obey Him without all our questions answered.

When it is difficult to surface the *Lesson* in a single step, surface clues for a while and eventually a *Lesson* will emerge.

Points of View

The next thing to try is to look at the passage from different points of view. You may have viewed the comic strip from the point of view of the one apologizing as we did above. If a *Lesson* is not coming from that perspective, then think of the story from the other person's point of view.

What *Lessons* could you learn from watching the other person? We can be trapped in anger if we refuse to forgive others. Forgiving benefits the victim the most because the aggressor still has to deal with his conscience.

The *Passage 1* homework can be viewed from the points of view of Abraham, Isaac and Jacob, Sarah, or God. From Isaac you can learn about how your world can be effected when God leads someone else in the family in a particular direction. From Sarah you can learn how God may allow barren times but He also can resolve them supernaturally.

When you have difficulty finding the Lesson, looking at the passage from different points of view will give you many more possibilities to consider.

Authors and Recipients

Keep in mind that every passage in the Bible is written by two authors and is written for two different recipients.

The two authors of every Bible passage are God and the human author. The human author of the passage might be someone like Paul, John, or Moses—whoever wrote that particular Bible book. The first of the two recipients are the ancient people, like the church at Ephesus or the Christians in Rome. We are the second recipient of every Bible passage.

So, as you look at the passage, consider the author/recipient combinations and ask yourself, "Why would the human author write this to the Galatians or why would God write this to us?" As you see the passage from these different vantage points, a *Lesson* will often present itself.

What is God Like?

If you can't find a *Lesson* using the other ideas, there is one thing you can always learn from any passage of scripture— you can always learn what kind of person God is.

To say that God is a person or that He has a personality is not to say that God is a human being. He is not finite in any way. Rather, we are saying that God has a personality. There are things He likes and things He does not like. He holds some values as more important than other values. Some things move Him and other things do not.

As you look at your passage, notice how God acts, what He values, and what concerns Him. Then ask yourself, "What kind of person would act this way or value this kind of thing." Begin to build a mental picture of what kind of person God is.

Our goal is to know Him better so we can love and trust Him more. God tells Abraham to step out without giving him a lot of details. From this we can see that God is a strong leader. He is not anxiously hovering over His followers reminding them what they need to do next or what to be aware of. He gives a command and feels secure. We can learn about God's personality by watching how He behaves.

When you have difficulty coming up with a *Lesson* in your passage, give these ideas a try. Most of the time the *Lessons* are right under our nose. We just need to look at the passage from a different perspective to see them.

"The expression of
Christian character
is not doing good,
but God-likeness."

Oswald Chambers

Appendix F
Answering Your Questions

Normally in devotional Bible study it is best to put your focus on the parts of the passage that make sense to you rather than focusing on what you don't understand. The purpose of devotional Bible study is to feed yourself rather than to solve every problem you encounter.

Picture for a moment a cow walking out into a rich pasture full of luscious food in every direction. But over in the corner is a patch of ground where the grass is not growing very well. Now, it would not make sense for the cow to rush over to the barren part of the field and spend all its time trying to eat the grass that is barely growing when it is surrounded by such available food.

In a similar way, when you open a passage to study it, there are usually a number of things that make sense and some things you don't understand. Learn to focus on the things that make sense and so feed yourself from the richness of the field rather than spending all your time looking at problems and coming away from your study without nourishing your soul.

How to Answer Your Questions

Having said that, there are some times that it is worth the distraction to resolve questions that come up. For example, if you are preparing to teach a Bible passage to a group of people, you should probably answer some of the questions that occur in the passage so you can answer the group's questions. Or if you encounter a question that prevents you from understanding the rest of the passage, that might be a good question to answer for yourself.

Once you have a question, it is sometimes unclear how you should go about answering it. Consider how children's questions are answered.

If you are a parent, or have been around children, you probably have had to answer a lot of questions. Many of the questions are on topics familiar to you, but some of them are on unfamiliar topics. Yet they still want an answer. So you probably do your best to piece together a likely answer.

For example, suppose a circus has come to town and you take a small child to watch the circus parade down the street. As you watch, a plate spinner goes by and a child asks how they do that. You may have to think for a minute or two. Then you might speculate that there is probably a groove in the bottom of the plate that the stick fits into. Or perhaps the plates stay stable because of the high speed at which they are spinning. As long as the plate is spun quickly and the stick remains in the middle, it works. One way or the other, you give your best guess and surprisingly, your best guess is often quite close.

Steps

When you have a question you want to answer, use the following steps to answer it.

1. Pray for Wisdom

It is surprising how often the answer to our question is right before our eyes in plain view but we don't see it. Pause, take some time. Ask God to open your eyes and help you see. He loves to give us wisdom *(James 1:5)* and He does open our eyes.

2. List All Possible Answers

Take a look at your question, take a look at the passage, and imagine as many answers as you can. The answers do not need to be perfectly supportable, they just need to be potential statements that would answer your question. If you work with it, you can usually come up with at least two or three possible answers.

If you can't think of any possibilities, then imagine the most persistent child you know is asking the question. This child will not take "I don't know" for an answer. Whatever you would tell that child is what you should write down.

This is a creative step. Take the leash off your mind and let it run freely and write down what you come up with.

3. Write Out the Support for Each Answer

Look at the first answer, then look at the passage and write down all the reasons that would support this being the answer to your question. Then do the same thing for each of the other possible answers.

At this point you are making an argument for each answer. Be as unbiased as you can. Surface everything you can see or think of that supports the answer.

4. Choose the Best Answer Based on the Support

Now sit back and survey the possible answers and their support. You are judge and jury. The Holy Spirit is opening your eyes. Decide for yourself, which answer has the greatest chance of being correct based on the strength of its support. That is the answer to your question.

5. Check an Authority

Once you have surfaced and weighed the evidence and have an opinion of your own, it is a good time to compare your opinion with the opinion of an authority or two.

You might use an online resource or go to a Christian bookstore and look for commentaries that cover your passage to see if they address your question. You might ask a pastor, or other church leader whose opinion you trust, what their answer would be to your question and why they favor that answer.

As you check with these authorities, if they cover your question and suggest an answer, be careful what you do with the answer. Do not discard your answer and adopt the authority's answer because the authority may have studied more than you.

Rather, go back to your list of possible answers and support for each answer and add the new information contributed by the authority. Now sit back and decide which answer seems right based on the strength of its support.

Remember, when you meet the Lord in heaven, He is not going to ask you what your pastor thinks. He is going to ask you what *you* think. Go with the answer that makes the most sense to *you*.

Can Anyone Do This?

When it comes to answering your own questions, some people worry they are not smart enough. In devotional Bible study, smartness is not the issue. Let me illustrate.

There was a popular eschatological scholar who went from town to town giving lectures on the end time events described in the Bible. He made a living untangling the complex imagery described in the books of Ezekiel, Daniel, and Revelation and explaining them to church congregations.

He arrived at a certain city to hold a week long conference on end time prophecy. During the week he had an appointment to meet someone at a local High School. As he walked through the school to find his appointment location, he passed by an open door that caught his attention. He had some time, so he stepped into the doorway to investigate.

He found himself in a large gymnasium. The gymnasium was empty except for an old humble janitor sitting on a bleacher on the other side of the room. What caught the conference speaker's attention was what the janitor had in his lap. It looked like he had a Bible.

The conference speaker crossed the room and came to the janitor and sat down. As he did, he was interested to notice the man was reading from the book of Revelation.

The speaker said to him, "I notice you are reading the book of Revelation. Do you understand what you are reading?" The elderly janitor replied, "Well, yes sir, I think I do." Intrigued, the scholar asked, "So tell me, what does it mean?" The janitor thought for a second then replied, "God wins in the end."

You don't have to be smart to understand the Bible. What God wants you to understand is simple enough for a child to understand (Matthew 19:14).

The Rest of the Answers?

Another worry that some people have about devotional Bible study, is how they will ever get the bulk of their questions answered if they don't focus on the things they don't understand. That is best explained by the following true illustration.

An experiment was conducted in a college level pottery class. The students were split into two groups. One group was told it would be graded solely on *how many* pots they made. The more they made, the higher their grade, regardless of the quality of the pots. The other group was told it would be graded solely on the *quality* of the pots it made.

At the end of the course the best pots from both groups were compared. Can you guess which group produced the highest quality pots? Logically you would expect the group that was graded on the quality of their pots to have the highest quality pots. However, the group that was graded on *how many* pots they made, was found to have the highest quality pots.

Practice makes perfect. The more you study the Bible, the more you come across the answers to your questions. Also, the more you grow, the fewer questions you will need answered and the more things you will trust God about. The more you study the Bible and grow in your walk with the Lord, the more your questions will be resolved.

"Practice
makes perfect."

The Authors

"It looks like
our schedules
are completely
unchangeable."

The Authors

Now it is time to discuss how to pick a time to do the Bible reading time you have designed. If you already have a time that works well for you, the chances are that at some point, your life circumstances will change and you will need to adjust your time slot again. The following ideas are helpful any time you need to select a time slot for your Time with God.

The Problem

Whenever we attempt to add a regular activity to our schedule there appears to be no room for it. We have already stretched our schedules to meet the demands of our modern lives.

It looks like our schedules are completely unchangeable. We have worked so hard to get our schedules to work as poorly as they do, we don't want to risk making things worse.

This kind of thinking is a problem because when you think like this you tend to rule out possible time slots without giving the necessary thought to what might be possible.

Some people address this problem by suggesting you put your Time with God anywhere in your schedule, then make that time work by raw dedication, determination, and perseverance. Others focus on the amount of time and suggest ways of trimming the time down so far that your Time with God fits into a crack in your schedule that is hardly noticeable.

For most people, neither of these approaches help their Time with God compete effectively with the demands of their busy life. The steps below do a better job of putting your Time with God in a place to succeed.

Steps

Select the Best Time of Day

Temporarily wipe your schedule completely clean. Pretend, for a minute, that you have no time commitments whatsoever.

Now, focus on the kind of activity you would like to do in your Time with God and identify what kind of energy it requires. When you think about the Bible reading time you designed in the last chapter, do you require high energy, meditative energy, peacefulness, or just an alert task orientation?

Once you have identified what kind of energy you would like, think through your day and see when that kind of energy is available. Is that kind of energy most likely available at noon time, late at night, or in the morning? Remember you have wiped your schedule clean. Your only concern is to discover when you have the kind of energy you need for your Time with God.

Select the Frequency that Matches Your Desire

After you have identified the ideal time of day for your Time with God, decide how much time each session should take and how many sessions to have each week.

To answer this question, you must consult the *Desire* you have been surfacing. You should select an amount of time that is enough to challenge you, but not too much to overwhelm your current *Desire*.

For some people that might be 2 or 3 times per week for 15-30 minutes each. The amount of time varies widely between individuals. The stronger your *Desire*, the more time it can support.

Don't make the mistake of trying to be immediately perfect. People frequently make this mistake when trying to add exercise to their schedule. They buy a gym membership and decide they will come every day for 1 hour. Most burn out within a few days because they overshoot their desire. Be honest with yourself. Find where your desire level is and start there. If you start where you are at, your *Desire* will grow.

Wrap Your Life Around It

Once you decide on the best time slots, dedicate yourself to finding a way to wrap your whole life around it.

Don't be fooled into assuming it is impossible to clear your ideal time slot. You are an adult. You have resources. You can make decisions that make things better. You have power and creativity.

It might mean you have to go to bed earlier and record TV shows for later viewing, or just stop watching some TV shows. It might mean you change how you eat lunch so you have time at lunch time. It might mean you go into work a bit later in the morning.

Example

I [N] went through these steps and decided I wanted my Time with God in the morning, but after I had my shower and breakfast so I would be awake.

So, I went to bed earlier, got up earlier, and had my Time with God after I got ready for work. But the whole time I kept thinking about all the cars that were piling onto the freeway ahead of me and how slow rush hour would be when I got there.

Then I decided I would leave the house early, get to work early, avoid rush hour, and have my Time with God in my office before others got there. Well, I avoided rush hour all right, but I just couldn't feel right having my Time with God in my office. After all, I was at work and I should be working.

At this point I had tried two things and they didn't work. Should I give up? No—I am an adult. I have resources. I can make decisions that improve my situation. So I kept thinking and experimenting.

If I was an *Extrovert*, my next step would be to figure out a way to have my Time with God in a fast food place like McDonald's. I could stay as long as I needed and I could write out the prayer portion of my Time with God.

But, as an *Introvert*, I ended up selling my beloved VW bug and bought a used cargo van which I converted into a surf van. I drove it to work early in the morning, got comfortable with pillows in the back and had my Time with God alone in the van before work. I got there before rush hour so avoided the traffic and had my own environment to enjoy my Time with God. The bonus was that I now had a way to surf at lunch time since I could carry my surfboard in the van and change in the back.

If you dare to think ideally, you will be surprised how close you can get your life to line up with your true values.

"I am an adult.
I have resources.
I can make decisions
that improve
my situation."

The Authors

"Create your
Time with God
like you choose
a cup of
Designer coffee"

The Authors

Designing a Time With God

How do you create a time with God that will match your current interests and *Desires*.

As I {N} think about creating a Time with God, I am reminded of the rise of *Designer* coffee drinks. For the longest time coffee drinkers only had a choice between having their coffee "black" or with "cream and sugar." But now there are so many options available that a person can practically create a drink that is unique to their personal tastes and current frame of mind. What's more, people become quite adamant about exactly how they like their coffee and will not accept anything less.

I would like you to put together your Time with God like you were selecting a *Designer* coffee drink. Don't think your only choice is to have it "black" or with "cream and sugar." Create a *Designer* Time with God that has incorporated your personality, interests, and current frame of mind.

As you begin to think about what would work for you, realize that a Time with God consists of two main areas: *Bible Study* and prayer. Any strategy should include something from both of these areas. You are looking for something that sounds interesting and challenging but does not overwhelm your *Desire*.

Let's first suggest some options for the *Bible Study* portion.

The Bible Study Portion

Here are several approaches to the *Bible Study* portion of your Time with God. The *FLCR* approach to *Bible Study* teaches you the core skills of *Bible Study* and develops your confidence in *Bible Study*. After you have learned *FLCR* if you find that it needs some adjusting to work best for you, by all means modify it to meet your needs. Remember that you are in charge of meeting your spiritual needs.

The sections that follow suggest several ways you can organize your Bible Study time. As you take a look at these suggestions, you are looking for something that intrigues you. If you pick something that sounds good for a while, but you eventually lose interest in it, progress from there to another suggestion that sounds interesting. A *Desire-led* Time with God puts a priority on monitoring the success of your time and continuing to adjust it to fit your current *Desire*.

Flicker a Bible Book

If *Flicker* is working well for you, then continue with it. If you are interested in studying Bible books from the beginning to the end (and your level of *Desire* can support that) I would suggest you study the books in the following order:

1. *Philippians*
2. *Galatians*
3. One of these: *Matthew, Mark, Luke, John*
4. *James*
5. *Genesis*
6. *Joshua*
7. *Psalms*
8. *1st* and *2nd Samuel*
9. *1st* Kings
10. *Proverbs*
11. *Romans*

This list proceeds from truth that is simplest and most directly applicable to the more complicated truth. It also provides a pretty good survey of Bible history and doctrine.

Your challenge will be to write *Facts* about each verse in your passage until something strikes you and you get a *Lesson*. Then make a *Challenge* from it and either continue to your *Response* and prayer time or go back to writing *Facts* on the following verses and repeat the process until you run out of time.

Basically I would recommend that you read until something hits you and go only as far as time permits.

God's Personality

If you are a "people person" you may like the kind of study that goes through the Bible to discover what kind of person God is.

To start this kind of study, you can go through the New Testament historical books like *Matthew, Mark, Luke, or John* to learn the personality of Jesus and thereby learn the personality of God since Jesus is God in the flesh.

Then you can study the Old Testament historical books like *Genesis, Exodus, Joshua, Judges, Ruth, 1 & 2 Samuel, 1 & 2 Kings, Nehemiah, and Esther* to learn the personality of God as God the Father interacts with humanity in general and with Israel in specific.

As you study, watch what God or Jesus reacts to. What makes Him joyful or angry, and what does He reward? Then consider what kind of person values those things and rewards those things?

In this kind of study you often have two different directions you can go. For example, if you are in a passage where people are having to wait before they receive what God has promised and you ask yourself, "What kind of person promises something then allows them to wait before giving it to them?" It might initially occur to you that mean people do that sort of thing and you might wonder if you should think God is mean?

When you come up with *bad* traits like this one, you should keep looking until you see a *good* quality trait. In this case as you looked at it more you would discover that this shows *good* quality traits like God is a strong and secure leader. He is not so insecure that He has to hover around people and prove Himself at every turn. He is the kind of secure person we all love to be around.*Topic*

Another approach is to study a topic of interest to you. You can do topical studies on subjects like: heaven, grace, anger, or forgiveness.

To find the verses that deal with your topic you can use a Topical Bible or Concordance if you have those kind of physical books. Or if you like to use your iPhone or iPad and have the *WAVE Parallel Bible* app you can use it to search for verses that have those words in them. Or if you like to use your home computer but don't have any special software, you can find verses on those topics by googling *Bible verses about heaven* or *Bible verses about grace*, etc.

Once you find the verses that deal with your topic, scan through them and select the verses you would like to *FLCR* and study the verses you have selected.

Biography

If you are a "people-person" you might enjoy studying some of the people in the Bible. There are many interesting characters like Joseph, Isaac, or David. If you interested in studying women of the Bible be sure to not miss Abigail. She is one of the wisest and pragmatic women of the Bible.

To find the verses that deal with the person you want to study, you can look up their name in a Topical Bible or Concordance if you have physical books like these. Or if you like to use your iPhone or iPad and have the *WAVE Parallel Bible* app you can use it to search for verses that have the name of your person in them. Or if you like to use your home computer but don't have any special software, you can find verses on individuals by googling *Bible verses about Joseph* or *Bible verses about Abigail,* etc.

Once you find the verses that deal with your person, scan through them and select the verses you would like to *FLCR* and study the verses you have selected.

Audio

You can even use the time you are in rush hour to commune with the Lord by listening to CD's of the Bible read aloud or CD's of devotional thoughts from the Bible.

The challenge in this kind of study is when and how to include prayer. You could wait until you get where you are going and pray before you get out of the car. Or you could try praying like Abraham did—out loud with your eyes open. Many of the Bible characters prayed with their eyes open. Closing your eyes just helps minimizes distractions.

If this kind of study appeals to you and challenges you, it can make use of some otherwise wasted moments in your day.

The Prayer Portion

The kind of prayer time you choose is highly dependent on what works best for you. Some people find it most natural to talk to God at the beginning of their time, some at the end, and some sprinkle it throughout the session. Some people spend a very short time in prayer and use most of their time in Bible study. Some do the exact opposite.

Try one approach and see how it goes. Adjust it as you go to fit what is currently the most motivating to you. Check

Chapter 7 and choose an aspect of prayer you would like to work on. Take responsibility for making the changes in your approach to find what is most helpful for you.

Do You Have a Winner?

As you are create your *Designer* Time with God, ask yourself the following three questions. Is your approach…

1. Enough to challenge you

2. Not too much to overwhelm your *Desire*

3. Something that intrigues you

If you can answer yes to all three questions, you have a winning design. If you can not answer yes to all three questions, adjust your design until you can.

"You are looking for
something that sounds
interesting and challenging
but does not
overwhelm your *Desire.*"

The Authors

"I suddenly
felt a passion
to do
follow-up work."

Noel

www.WaveStudyBible.com

More About the Authors

When we teach in person, we share more of our background story. For those who find this helpful, our story follows.

Early Years

Both of us were born in 1951, have been married since 1972, and have four grown kids.

We met in our Junior year at California Polytechnic University in San Luis Obispo, California. Denise was a speech major and had recently accepted the Lord through the Campus Crusade for Christ ministry. I [N] was a mechanical engineering major and became a Christian during my childhood. I had rededicated my life to the Lord in a little Baptist church just off campus.

One Sunday I was singing in the choir when Denise and her two roommates walked in and sat in the back. OK, so I found myself distracted by the glow coming from that side of the room.

At the end of the service, the minister invited anyone who had recently accepted Jesus as their Savior to come to the front of the room. Denise came forward and I suddenly felt a passion to do follow-up work. I became the answer to her prayer for Christian fellowship and we were married the next summer.

School

We felt called into the ministry and left Cal Poly for Baptist Bible College of Pennsylvania. In our four years there, I earned a Bachelors in Bible and taught classical guitar on the faculty. Denise also earned a Bachelors in Bible there.

Since all the good teachers at the school were from Dallas Theological Seminary, after graduating we moved to Dallas to attend DTS. All four of our kids were born in Dallas. According to our two year old, I attended the "Dallas *Theo-laundromat* Seminary."

Both Denise and I tackled the challenging programs of DTS. She pursued a Masters in Bible but stopped half way through after delivering our twins. In Bible college I concentrated on Greek, so in DTS I completed a Th.M. in Hebrew Exegesis.

After graduation while still in Dallas, I enjoyed a ministry at Dallas Bible College where I taught, Bible, theology, guitar, and Introduction to Computers. I also worked on staff at Dallas Theological Seminary.

Computer and Teaching

When I [N] graduated from DTS, I had an interesting and significant twist in direction.

While I was working on the DTS staff they had a need for someone who knew computers. I had an engineering and programming background from Cal Poly and got the position. In this responsibility I eventually created and managed DTS's mainframe data center and started programming the *WAVE Parallel Bible®* app in the evenings.

After being out of state for 15 years the Lord led us back to our roots in Southern California. I got a programming job and advanced in the computer field. After a number of years I was a Chief Architect for AOL doing research and development. During that time, I earned patent #20030208543 for inventing Video Messaging, Prentice Hall published my book on Java programming, and I taught Java programming at UC Irvine extension.

Depression and Recovery

For one reason or another I [N] had an emotionally difficult childhood. During that time I made coping decisions that were appropriate for that situation but not appropriate for adult life. When I grew up, I did not update those decisions and eventually they caught up with me. While I was working for Dallas Theological Seminary I landed in the hospital with a clinical depression. The three weeks I was in the hospital brought my life to a complete stand still.

During that time I had no idea what God was doing in my life. All I knew was, if I was going to get out of this, it was going to require a lot of work on my part. Regardless of my devotion to God, He was allowing these dynamics to shut down my life and the only way back was to tackle them head on.

So, with counseling and the skillful and kind support of Denise, I surfaced the flawed coping decisions made as a child and updated them. This was a difficult task that demanded all of my creativity and brought most of my ministry activities to a stop.

During this time, I was focused on emotional recovery, meeting the needs of our family, and my job. The little time I was able to give to ministry took the form of teaching people to study the Bible and programming the *WAVE Parallel Bible.*®

After a decade, things returned to an even keel and I finished my schooling by earning a Doctor of Education specializing in Internet-based learning systems which found their way into the *WAVE Parallel Bible.*®

Psychology and Private Practice

After the kids were older, Denise went back and got her Masters and Doctor of Psychology degrees and opened a clinical private practice. Her specialty is integrating Biblical principles with principles of good mental health.

WAVE Study Bible® Ministry

The first influence toward the *WAVE Study Bible® Ministry* occurred several years ago when a young married woman in our church asked Denise if she would mentor her. She wanted to know how to love the Lord better and be a good wife. The material Denise delivered to the woman and a group of her friends was so well-received that Denise gave the course to several other groups in the church.

Then God gave us a special moment as we were applying the teaching of our church's course on spiritual gifts. We were trying to find a ministry that would make use of our combined gifts and God stopped us in our tracks. He gave us the idea to combine our ministries to help people with their Bible reading times.

Denise's discipleship and psychology background helped address the motivational issues that stop most Bible reading times. My background teaching people how to study the Bible addressed the skills that are needed for Bible reading. The combination of addressing motivation along with skill development has proven to be especially effective.

When God led me into the computer field in 1981, it felt like a diversion and did not make much sense. But soon after I entered this field, God gave me the idea to develop software that taught people how to study the Bible. Today the Internet age has arrived and, the *WAVE Parallel Bible®* is ready. It has been exciting to see how this tool has helped people study and share what they are learning with others. What seemed like a diversion, got me working on a tool that was ready in time to leverage the resources of the Internet.

After the idea for the combined ministry was born, we wrote this book and taught it to hundreds of people in churches in our area. As we did, we experienced the kind of ministry we envisioned many years ago when we set out for Bible College. Now the *WAVE Study Bible® Ministry* has grown to involve many people and has a wide reach.

Our life has taken many turns and twists and has defied conventional wisdom. But, as always, God's path has brought us directly to His will and we are thankful for His work in our lives.

CPSIA information can be obtained
at www.ICGtesting.com
Printed in the USA
FSHW010507110919
61908FS